ROYAL EÓGHANACHT SOCIETY PUBLICATIONS

Cashel '96

Three Centuries of Niadh Nask Bookplates

Links in a Golden Chain

A New Book of Rights (Leabhar na gCeart Nua)

Justin MacCarthy, Lord Mountcashel

The Kings of the Race of Eibhear

ROYAL EÓGHANACHT SOCIETY
PO Box 70, Clonmel, County Tipperary, Ireland

The Kings of the Race of Eibhear

The Kings of the Race of Eibhear
A CHRONOLOGICAL POEM

by
JOHN O'DUGAN (circa 1370)
[Seán Óg Ó Dubhagáin]

Translated by
MICHAEL KEARNEY (1635)

Edited by
JOHN DALY (1847)

With a Foreword
by
PETER BERRESFORD ELLIS

Commentary and Appendices
by
THE MacCARTHY MÓR, PRINCE OF DESMOND

A ROYAL EÓGHANACHT SOCIETY PUBLICATION

Copyright © 1999 The Royal Eóghanacht Society

ALL RIGHTS RESERVED. EXCEPT AS PERMITTED UNDER THE UNITED STATES COPYRIGHT ACT, 1976, NO PART OF THE PUBLICATION MAY BE REPRODUCED OR DISTRIBUTED IN ANY FORM OR BY ANY MEANS, OR STORED IN A DATA BASE OR RETRIEVAL SYSTEM, WITHOUT THE PERMISSION OF THE AUTHORS.

Library of Congress Cataloging-in-Publication Data

O'Dugan, John
    The Kings of the Race of Eibhear, A Chronological Poem by John O'Dugan [Seán Óg Ó Dubhagáin](circa 1370), Translated by Michael Kearney (1635), Edited by John Daly (1847); with a foreword by Peter Berresford Ellis; Commentary and Appendices by The MacCarthy Mór, Prince of Desmond - 1st edition.
    ISBN: 0-9654220-6-2

Published by:
Gryfons Publishers and Distributors
P.O. Box 1899
Little Rock, Arkansas 72203-1899 U.S.A.
gryfons.hypermart.net
ballywoodn@aol.com
facsimile 501-834-4038

Layout and Typesetting:
David Robert Wooten of Ballywoodane
   NN, OMNN, MRES, FRSAI, FSA(Scot)

Typesetting and Proofreading:
Dr. Patrick Michael O'Shea of Tiraha
   NN, Ollamh of Music, FRES, BMus, MMus, DMA

First Edition
10 9 8 7 6 5 4 3 2 1

MULTUM IN PARVO
An Foilsitheoir Ríoga
By Appointment to the Eóghanacht Royal House of Munster

ACKNOWLEDGMENTS

I am grateful to The Count of Clandermond for assisting me in the historical research upon which my Commentary is based, and to An t'Ollamh Peter Berresford Ellis for providing the Foreword. I should also like to thank An t'Ollamh Dr. Patrick M. O'Shea of Tiraha for proofreading my text, and David Robert Wooten of Ballywoodane for typesetting it.

Finally, it is appropriate for me, on behalf of the Royal Eóghanacht Society, to acknowledge the financial assistance of The O'Donoghue of the Glens, NN, and the Royal Eóghanacht Foundation Incorporated, without whom this book could not have been published.

The MacCarthy Mór, Prince of Desmond
Cashel, January 1999.

THE ROYAL EÓGHANACHT SOCIETY

The Royal Eóghanacht Society was founded in 1996 by The MacCarthy Mór, Prince of Desmond, during the quatercentenary commemoration of the death of King Donal IX MacCarthy Mór, last regnant King of Desmond and titular King of Munster.

The specified purposes of the Society are to encourage an academic interest in the history of Eóghanacht Munster, publish material relevant to that period, and to preserve heirlooms associated with the MacCarthy Mór Dynasty.

The Statutes provide for the appointment of no more than ten fellows and twenty-five members each of whom must have rendered conspicuous service in an intellectual field to the Eóghanacht Dynasty. There are no membership fees and appointment is for life.

To The O'Donoghue of the Glens,
a Gaelic Chief in fact and not only in name,
in whose veins flows the royal blood of Milesius,
Eibhear and Eóghan Mór.

CONTENTS

Foreword
    Peter Berresford Ellis _____ i

The Kings of the Race of Eibhear
    Reproduction of Original Text _____ 1

Commentary
    The MacCarthy Mór, Prince of Desmond _____ 33

Appendix I
    A Successional List of the Kings of Munster _____ 53

Appendix II
    Genealogical Charts of the Eóghanacht and
    Dal gCais Kings of Munster _____ 57

Appendix III
    The Descent of Conall Corc from Eibhear and Milesius _____ 65

Appendix IV
    Notes on John Daly's Preface to the 1847 Edition _____ 69

FOREWORD
by
Peter Berresford Ellis
NN, BA(Hons), MA, FRES, FRSAI, FRHistS

In considering the genealogies of Gaelic kings and princes, the first thing that strikes one is the fact that the records are so numerous. The first major surviving genealogy is to be found in the Bodleian Library, Oxford, listed as Rawlinson MS B 502, a twelfth-century work which is the earliest surviving manuscript to contain complete Brehon law tracts. It was this genealogical work that was the basis for the *Corpus Genealogiarum Hiberniae* (vol. i) edited by M.A. O'Brien, Dublin, 1962. However, the twelfth-century genealogies, like the surviving texts of Irish law, demonstrate that they are copies, or incorporations, of material that had been first written down in the seventh century.

Professor Eoin MacNeill, examining the fifteenth-century MS Laud Misc 610, a manuscript of genealogies, demonstrated that it was a copy of an eleventh-century book written at Armagh. ('Notes on the Laud Genealogies,' *Zeitschrift für celtische Philologie* 8 (1911) pp. 411-418.

Dr. Douglas Hyde, in his *Literary History of Ireland* (T. Fisher Unwin, London, 1899) writes on the subject:

> The whole intricate system of Irish genealogy, jealously preserved from the very first, as all Irish literature goes to show, played so important a part in Irish national history and in Irish social life, and is at the same time so intimately bound up with the people's traditions and literature, and throws so much light upon the past, that it will be well to try to get a grip of this curious and intricate subject, so important for all who would attempt to arrive at any knowledge of the life and feelings of the Irish and Scottish Gael, and upon which so much formerly depended in the history and alliances of both races.

In a dispassionate look at the history of genealogical records in Ireland, scholars can be agreed that these records were not written down until the start of the Christian period, particularly when the Irish *ollamhain* decided to adopt the Latin alphabet to start making their extensive accounts. The surviving works, dating from the twelfth century were copies of earlier works and, in modern parlance, 'updates' of preceding works. Large parts of the *Leabhar na Nuachomghbhala* or *Book of Leinster*, compiled by Fionn MacGormain about 1150; the *Book of Ballymote*, compiled in 1390 by Maghnus Ó Duibhgeánáin, the *Book of Lecan*, compiled by Giolla Íosa Mór Mac Firbis about 1400, all contain genealogies. These books are well known.

i

However, less well known are many other medieval works on genealogy, some contained in Trinity College, Dublin, labelled simply as MSS H.3.28 and H.2.4. There are many other manuscript books such as the genealogies of the Eugenians, the Book of Meath, Book of Connellians, Book of Oriel and others. All these works were the product of scholars working with earlier material. Perhaps one of the last surviving works in this tradition was the massive compilation made by Dubhaltach Mac Firbisigh (1585-1670) of Sligo known as 'Genealogies of the Families of Ireland,' part of which was published as *Genealogies, Tribes and Customs of Hy-Fiachrach*, commonly called O'Dowd's Country, translated with notes by John O'Donovan, Dublin 1844. MacFirbisigh, one of the great Irish scholars of the time, had to seek protection in the house of Sir James Ware in Dublin during the height of the Cromwellian persecutions. He survived. However, on a journey from his home in 1670 he met a young English soldier who murdered him.

We can argue, therefore, that Irish genealogists used written records from the seventh century at least, but Irish genealogies stretch back even beyond this period to the arrival of the sons of Golamh, known as 'the soldier of Spain' - Míle Easpain or Milesius - which places us at the end of the second millennium before Christ. This is beyond the scope of our known written records, so how can we be sure that these early records are correct? Most genealogies go back to Anno Mundi 2737; Anno Mundi being based on AM 1 as the date of the creation of the world, a system used in many early Christian texts. In the Hebrew tradition the year of creation corresponds to 3761 BC which would make the date of the arrival of the Milesians in Ireland to be 1024 BC. Even if we accept the computation given by the Archbishop of Armagh, James Ussher (1581-1656), a Dublin graduate of Trinity College, who became its Professor of Theological Controversies, the Milesian settlement in Ireland would have taken place in 1267 BC. Whether we believe this method of dating or not, it is becoming fairly certain that there was a new settlement of Continental Celts in Ireland around the end of the second millennium BC, and this is actually substantiated by recent archaeological finds showing a new Continental technology arriving in Ireland around this period.

If the first genealogies were not committed to writing until about the fifth, sixth and seventh centuries, this would mean that the oral tradition of transmitting the information had to be sustained well over one thousand five hundred years. Needless to say, conservative scholarship gives little credit to oral traditions and anything before the seventh century AD in Ireland is dismissed as 'pseudo history.' As an aside, I have always wondered why we are so keen to accept, as utterly incontrovertible and without challenge, every word of Julius Caesar's *Commentaries* when the earliest surviving versions of his work we have only date from the ninth century AD, yet, at the same time, we decry Irish histories referring to earlier periods as 'pseudo'? Can it be the result of our curious prejudice against native Irish records compared with the centuries of propaganda of the accuracy and civilising nature of the Graeco-Roman records?

Without attempting to be ironic, however, we can, in this instance, accept the Graeco-Roman comments on early Celtic society which inform us that the Celts had a impressive and impeccable tradition of committing to memory immense amounts of knowledge and passing it on in oral tradition.

For a long time now, I have argued that the oral traditions of any culture are worthy of respect. I have witnessed several times how oral tradition can be an accurate source of material. In 1985 I was in Buffalo, New York, researching on the Irish Republican Brotherhood's invasion of British North America at the end of the American Civil War. In a local Buffalo newspaper, the *Buffalo Courier*, for June, 1866, there was a passing two line reference to a band of Native Americans, from an Iroquois reservation, volunteering to join the IRB force. Intrigued, wanting to know more, I was directed to a Reservation just south of Buffalo, beyond Lackawana, where, in the Holy Cross Cemetery of Lackawana, many graves of Irishmen who gave their lives in that venture are to be found. I was directed to a very elderly man who, it was said, was the tribe's oral historian. I watched with awe that oral tradition at first hand.

The old man calculated how many generations it had been since 1866; then he smiled and out came the name of the tribal chief and his war chief, and then he recited by heart a half-dozen sentences relating to the incident which confirmed and enhanced the throwaway lines printed in the Buffalo Courier that June of 1866. My studies in this respect were published in *The Irish Sword*, (Journal of the Military History Society of Ireland) Vol. XVI No. 65 and Vol. XVIII No. 73.

Returning, though, to the more ancient oral traditions, I have expressed my views of Celtic oral traditions in my study *The Druids* (Constable, London, 1994) and, in this respect, in my section on 'Druids as Historians' (pp 199 ff.). The accuracy of Celtic oral tradition can actually be seen in a reference in Tacitus when he comments that in AD 69 the Gaulish Druids knew the story of the Celtic sack of Rome c. 390/387 BC which had been made by a Celtic tribe who had then settled on the Italian peninsular. The history of that tribe had been transmitted to the heartland of Gaul and remembered after four centuries in oral tradition. The same tradition occurred among the British Celts even to a later period and thus could Geoffrey of Monmouth recite that tradition in his epic *Historia regum Britanniae*.

We can be sure that Irish learning was being carefully transmitted, generation to generation, in much the same way as every other culture had used before the advent of the writing form. Usually, these matters were handed down in poetic form. Professor Myles Dillon has pointed out: "The prose-and-verse form is also the oldest Indian narrative form, and in Sanskrit we have examples which show how heroic epic grew out of a verse dialogue ... the verse epic of ancient India and Homer's *Iliad*." That this form was also part of Irish tradition, indeed, the wider Celtic tradition, needs little confirmation.

At the time when the Irish law system was being codified, the *Senchus Mór* states that the qualified historian, or *ollamh*, had to be specially learned in chronology, synchronism, antiquities and genealogy. He or she had to know at least 350 histories and romance tales by heart and be able to recite them word perfect at a moment's notice. An *ollamh* was supposed to know the prerogatives, rights, duties, restrictions and tributes not only of the High King but all the provincial and petty kings. The *Leabhar na gCeart* (Book of Rights) states: 'The learned historian who does not know the prerogatives and prohibitions of these kings, is not entitled to visitations or to sell his composition.'

An interesting parallel to the office of *seanchaí*, who were the keepers of these old traditions, especially the genealogies, occurs in Ireland's sister Indo-European culture - Hindu society. A class of poets called *sutras* or court poets who also acted as charioteers for the warriors, often kept the genealogical accounts. The charioteer in Hindu society was the intimate friend of the warrior and we find just such a relationship between charioteers and warriors in Irish society. In Irish saga the charioteers extolled the prowess of their warriors. The Sanskrit *Satapatha Brahmana* says that on the evening of the first day of the horse sacrifice (and horse sacrifice is known in ancient Irish kingship rituals) the poets had to chant a praise poem in honour of the king or his warriors, usually praising his genealogy and deeds.

Professor Dillon points out that this praise poetry is found in the *Rigveda* and is called *narasayah* 'praise of the warrior.' Similarly such praise poems are found in Irish sources. Professor Dillon points to the Leinster king, Labraid Loingsech, and identifies a long poem of this kind, called *fursundud*. The name in Old and Middle Irish specifically applied to a genealogical praise poem to exalt the princes of a certain dynasty. The word has the implication of illuminating, throwing light on, setting forth clearly. It comes from the same root as *fursaintid*, the order of the third degree of wisdom of an *ollamh*. Professor Dillon adds that many such poem genealogies, written for the Eóghanacht Kings, also survive. Professor Dillon says:

> I suggest that these oldest Irish poems are true *narasayah* (they date from a time before the classical Irish metres had developed, some of them before the use of rhyme), and that they were sung at the king's consecration, and on so solemn an occasion as the holding of the Feast of Tara by the High King.

Therefore the *fursundud* of Irish poem-genealogies, like the *narasayah* in Sanskrit, both have their roots in a common Indo-European form and their origin is lost in the mists of the primordial development of that culture. In the written form of the early Christian period, they were already the product of over 1,500 years of oral transmission. The early Christian scribes felt obligated to add to the genealogies an ancestry tracing Milesius' pedigree back twenty-two generations to Fenius Farsaidh, who 'devised the Irish language' at the time of the Tower of Babel, and naming him as a son of Baath. From there a further fourteen generations were added to take the ancestry back to Seth, a son of Adam. But this does not detract from the accuracy of the subsequent

Gaelic genealogies. It was merely the traditional thing to do in the early years of Christianity to ensure that the King could claim an accepted link with the origins of the religion of the people. Graeco-Roman writers point out that in the pre-Christian period the Celtic nobles traced their descent to the ancient gods and goddesses.

The poem of Seán Mór Ó Dubhagáin is a traditional *fursundud*.

It is an exceptional pleasure to write a foreword to the publication by the Royal Eóghanacht Society of Ó Dubhagáin's *fursundud* for the Eóghanacht Kings. I first came across the poem, in fact, some years ago in Cambridge University Library (Mss. Add.3084), amongst a pile of material, bearing on its cover, in pencil, the words 'Irish Poems & historical Genealogies.' The MS. was classified as 'Genealogies of the Munster kings.' I noted down the reference and first line '*Corca mc Luidhgheach mc Ailellae Flainn bicc...*' ending with the name of the author. At the time, I had no idea that other versions had survived nor that it had even been translated and published. I merely meant to return to the poem at a later date.

To be honest, I was more interested in chasing some references to a small number of elegies in Irish on Donal IX MacCarthy Mór (d. 1596). Some elegies had been written circa 1665 by Diarmuid Óg Ó Murchadha and yet another was dated 1730 under the name 'Eoghan Ua Súilleabháin.' This creates a mystery as the Munster poet Eoghan Ruadh Ó Súilleabháin was not born until 1748. Therefore we must be dealing with another Munster poet of the same name. However, I digress although I would be happy to pass on this puzzle to some other worker in the field.

The author of the poem under consideration, Ó Dubhagáin, flourished in the fourteenth century and is said to have died c. 1372. Yet the curious thing is that he was not a Munster poet at all but a Connachtman who was Chief Poet to the Ó Ceallaigh (O'Kelly) of Hy-Maine, whose country lay in the area of modern Counties Galway and Roscommon. How did this Connacht *file* come to have such an incredible knowledge of Eóghanacht kingship such as is displayed in his work? As The MacCarthy Mór shows us in his commentary, the poet displays a detailed knowledge of the succession details of the Kings of Munster over a period of a thousand years, missing out only minor figures who reigned as 'co-kings' or 'kings with opposition.' Moreover, the poet refers to the fathers of the various kings demonstrating an awareness of their genealogies.

Dr. Hyde does not mention this fact in his consideration of the poet's work, nor does he mention the poem itself, but prefers to comment on Ó Dubhagáin's other great work on topography, translated and edited by John O'Donovan in 1862. Dr. Hyde says that the poet was working on his topographical poem when he died **and before he was able to finish his researches on Munster** and it was therefore left to a young contemporary - Gilla-na-Naomh Ó hUidrin (d. 1420) to complete the section on the southern kingdoms. Alas, we know next to nothing about Ó hUidrin.

How credible is Dr. Hyde's claim? Why would the fact that a work was unfinished at the time of the poet's death imply that Ó Dubhagáin lacked the knowledge to finish it? We are all guilty of making ill-considered statements which do not hold up upon reflection.

Three points about Ó Dubhagáin's knowledge of Munster do not seem to have previously been made clear. We know that Ó Dubhagáin was Chief Poet to the O'Kelly of Hy Maine. The particular O'Kelly he was patronised by was William Boy (Liam Buidhe) O'Kelly who had married the daughter of O'Grady of Kiballyowen. This lady, while not exactly Eóghanacht was certainly Dál gCais, and she would be bound to have some knowledge of Thomond if not Munster kingship succession. She might even have taken Ua Bríain poets with her to Hy Maine in her personal retinue. The second point is that this same William Boy, in 1351, invited all the chief bards and musicians of Ireland to spend that Christmas at his court in a great bardic celebration. This is the origin of the Irish expression 'O'Kelly's welcome.' Ó Dubhagáin, as Chief Poet at the court, would have had place of prominence at such a gathering and what an opportunity it was to have personal contact with the Eóghanacht *ollamhain*! The third point is that at the time Ó Dubhagáin was writing he undoubtedly had access to a vast store of written records in Irish. We tend these days to forget just how many manuscript books were lost in those terrible devastations of the late sixteenth and through the seventeenth centuries. Vast Irish libraries have been destroyed.

Bearing these matters in mind, I would argue that there is little cause for surprise that Ó Dubhagáin could have produced this great *fursundud* for the Eóghanacht kings.

THE

KINGS OF THE RACE OF EIBHEAR.

A Chronological Poem,

BY JOHN O'DUGAN, WITH A TRANSLATION BY
MICHAEL KEARNEY, A.D. 1635.

EDITED

BY JOHN DALY.

DUBLIN:
JOHN DALY, 25, ANGLESEA-STREET.
1847.
Price One Shilling.

THE

KINGS OF THE RACE OF EIBHEAR.

A Chronological Poem,

BY JOHN O'DUGAN, WITH A TRANSLATION BY
MICHAEL KEARNEY, A. D. 1635.

EDITED

BY JOHN DALY.

DUBLIN:
JOHN DALY, 25, ANGLESEA-STREET.
1847.

Printed by Webb and Chapman, Great Brunswick-street.

Ríoġa ril Eibir

aġus fais a b-flaiċeas aṅ Leaċ Ṁhoġa.

Seaáṅ Ua Dúbhaġaiṅ, (John O'Dugan,) author of the following poem, was chief poet to O'Ceallaiġ (O'Kelly*) of Uí Ṁaiṅe, *(Ibh, or Hy Maine,)* which comprises a large territory within the present counties of Galway and Roscommon, extending from the Shannon at Lanesborough to the county of Clare, and from Athlone to Athenry in the county of Galway.

He wrote many poems besides that now for the first time given to the public, which gives a catalogue of the kings of Caireal, (Cashel,) and the years that each prince reigned, from its foundation by Coṅc, son of Luġaiḋ, about A.D. 380, to Toirḋealbaċ O'briaiṅ, (Turlogh O'Brien,) A.D. 1367. Mr. Edward O'Reilly, in his "Chronological Account of Irish Writers," a work which should be in the hands of every Irish scholar, mentions this poem fourth in his list of the author's historical and topographical pieces. He also enumerates the following, viz:

1—A poem of five hundred and sixty-four verses, beginning " Aṫá ruṅḋ reaṅċur ríoġ Ereaṅḋ." " Here is a History of the Kings of Eire."

This poem gives a catalogue of the kings of Ireland, from Sláiṅġe of the Fir-Bolg race, who, conjointly with his

---

* For the history of this great family, see Mr. O'Donovan's "Tribes and Customs of Hy-Many," published by the Irish Archæological Society.—A.D., 1843.

four brothers, Ꝥann, Ꝥeanann, Seanꝁann, and Ruꝺraiꝺe, sons of Deala Mac Loich, began to reign over Ireland, A.M. 2245, to Ruꝺraiꝺe O'Concubair, (Roderick O'Conor,) son of Toirꝺealbac Mor, (Turlogh the Great,) who held the reins of government in Ireland at the Anglo-Norman invasion, A.D. 1168.

2—A topographical and historical poem of eight hundred and eighty verses, beginning, "Triallam timceall na Foꝺla." "Let us go around Fodhla," (Ireland.) This poem gives the names of the principal tribes and districts in Meath, Ulster, and Connaught, and the chiefs who presided over them at the time Henry II. king of England, was invited to the country by Diarmuiꝺ Mac Murcaꝺa, King of Leinster.

3—A poem of two hundred and twenty-four verses, beginning, "Rioꝼraiꝺ Laiꝼean clann Chataoir." "Kings of Leinster, descendants of Cathaoir;" written on the families descended from Cataoir Mor, monarch of Ireland A.D. 174, to A.D. 177.

5—A poem of three hundred and thirty-two verses, beginning, "Teamair na rioꝼ rait Cormaic." "Tara of the kings, fortress of Cormac;" which gives an account of the battles and principal actions of Cormac mac Airt, monarch of Ireland in the middle of the third century.

6—A poem beginning, "Bliaꝺain ro rolur a ꝺat." "This year bright its dye:" written upon the festivals of the year, with practical rules for finding the moveable feasts and fasts, by the Epacts, Dominical Letters, &c.

7—A poem of two hundred and ninety-two verses, beginning, "Forur focal luaiꝺtear lib." "A knowledge of words spoken by you;" being a vocabulary of now obsolete words, and words, which, though spelled alike, have different, and often contrary meanings.

The Four Masters record the death of our bard under the year 1372. It is my wish to place all these poems in the hands of my countrymen, and it is my earnest hope, that those who may have copies of any of them will place the same in my hands, and thus aid me in the task I have now commenced. They form an interesting portion of our history, and, no doubt, the publication of them will tend to throw much light upon the neglected ancient literature and topography of Ireland.

That which I now present to the reader, I found in an unpublished manuscript translation of Dr. Keating's "Foꞃuꞃ Feaꞃa aꞃ Eꞃꞇꞃṅ;" made by a celebrated scribe, "Michael Kearney, of Ballyloskye, in the County of Crosse Tipperary;" who, being a contemporary of his learned author, began the task, A.D. 1635, which he brought to a successful close in 1668; it was purchased by me at the sale of the late Colonel Howard's library, at Mr. Sharpe's, Anglesea-street, and is now in the hands of a gentleman in this city.

This fine volume contains also many important historical references interspersed throughout its antique pages, in the shape of copious extracts from Leabaꞃ ꞃa c-Ceaꞃꞇ, (Book of Rights, now in course of publication by the Celtic Athenæum,) in the Leabaꞃ Leacaꞃ, (Book of Leacan,) a folio vellum MS. of the fifteenth century, which appears, in Kearney's time, to have been in Lower Ormond, in Tipperary, but which is now deposited in the valuable library of the Royal Irish Academy: also, from the Wars and Battles of Ceallacaꞃ Caꞇꞃl, with important researches into Irish history from the translator's own pen.

I cannot at present trace Kearney's history, but Ballyloskye, I am told, lies about three miles below the town of Nenagh; the ruins of an ancient castle, known as "Kearney Castle," stands close to the place, which possibly may have been the seat of the indefatigable translator of Dr. Keating's Foꞃuꞃ Feaꞃa, but now no trace of that name is found in that locality.

Although adopting his copy as my text, I have not done so, without carefully comparing it with another version from the pen of a Munster bard, Owen O'Keeffe, (afterwards the Rev. Owen O'Keeffe, of whom I may have occasion to speak more fully heareafter,) made in 1684; and which contains several additional stanzas, which will be found as the concluding portion of the poem. In the body of the poem, wherever the readings differed in an important particular, O'Keeffe's version will be found at the foot of the page. O'Reilly says, our poem contains 296 lines, *i. e.* 74 stanzas. In Kearney's copy there are only 64 stanzas in English, and there are 62 stanzas in Irish, interlined, apparently by Muꞃꞇꞃ mac Toꞃꞃa Uꞇ Mꞇhaoꞇl-Coꞃaꞇꞃe. O'Keeffe's copy contains 76 stanzas, one of which I have introduced [in brackets] in page 22; both copies correspond nearly to the bottom of page 26, and from that to the end O'Keeffe's copy proceeds as in pages 28 and 30.

O'Reilly in the work quoted above, (page 101,) says, that " a fine copy of this poem is in the Book of Ballymote, fol. 36, *a*, col. 2; and another in the collection of the Assistant Secretary," *i. e.* in his own possession; which I suppose to be now deposited, with the Book of Ballymote, in the library of the Royal Irish Academy.

The strict rules and conditions, upon which access to the manuscripts is permitted, are said to be imposed in the Academy, with the view to exclude such persons as would be likely to injure them, or to make an improper or dishonest use of their contents; but the real effect of them is, to exclude those humble Irish scholars who arrive in Dublin, from time to time, from the remote Irish districts; and who are of course friendless in the metropolis, as they are unpatronized; and as to the imputation about making an improper or dishonest use of the contents of manuscripts written many centuries back, I can form no idea what it means. So far as preventing injury or securing the safety of the property goes, it is very just; but I am told, that in the British Museum the freest access and every accommodation is given to any person who enters; as is done also in the libraries abroad; and, even in Marsh's ancient library in this city, the valuable collection there, of MSS. as well as printed books, is open to any literary person who wishes to avail himself of their contents; and there is only a single attendant, who would of course prevent any injury, if any thing so vile were attempted.

The Book of Ballymote is said to have been presented to the Royal Irish Academy, gratuitously, by the Chevalier O'Gorman, and not long since, £600 were voted by Parliament towards purchasing the collection of Irish manuscripts gathered by Messrs. Hodges and Smith, and other sums were raised among the public generally; but the booksellers, publishers, and others of Dublin have not had the benefit of the purchase.

The regulations are not suited to the wants of those who most need access to the manuscripts for study, information, and publication, the means of which ought to be as free as possible, the safety of the property being secured; certainly not more restricted than in the British Museum.

Kearney introduces his translation with the following brief remarks:

"Though (Reader) the subsequent Duaine, or Traine of Irish verses, made by O'Dowgaine, (y[e] most renowned Chronicler of Ireland in his own time,) bee not expressed by Father Geffery Keathing, the author of my present translation, in his Irish Chronicle, yet sith therein I find what is exp[E]ssed of the other side hereof touching the magnificiency and greatenesse of the Kings of Cashell anciently in this kingdom, obserued, I hope for the expression of the kings thereof for succession since the originall discovery of that famous place, now adorned with the Sea of the most Illustrious Arch[B]pp. and Metropolitane of Mounster, and Primate of Ireland, I shall passe excused for incerting the same traine of verses with my own inversion of them into English, in this present history of the remarkablest Antiquityes of this oppressed Nation, and that free from yo[E] blame, or exceptions, which is all the reward that for my paynes herein taken, I crave; and therevpon, p[E]suming vpon yo[E] good acceptance (not as an addition to the worke) but to preserue that ancieut Rhyme from the overwhelmeing flouds of oblivion, which already devoured most part of our Nationall Memoraryes; I offer it as I found the same in an ancient Manuscript, deserving y[w] of kindnesse, if by a perfecter Coppie thereof appeareing, yow find any thing hereing misreported, or misplaced, yow favourably rectifye the mistake or omission by mee in this beehalfe vnwillingly committed."

Seáan, mac Éamoinn, mic Dhomnaill Uí Dhálaigh.

Baile Átha Cliat,
Lá Bealltaine, m.d.ccc.xlvii.

Ríoġa ríl Eíbír, ⁊c.

Ua Dubaġáin, cc.

Cairiol caċair clann Moḋa,
port oiniġ ar eaġnaṁa;
port ríoġ na n-donn-brat maiseaċ,[1]
o Ċorc ġo Corbmac Cléireaċ.[2]

Do cloinn Moḋa Oilíll Oll,
níor ṡuiḋ a c-Caireal craob córr;
Eoġan Mór noċar an air,
ġlan a ġlór ór ġaċ ġarriaḋ.[3]

Cian Cúil-ḟionn ar Cormac Cas,
níor ċoġraḋ Cairiol claḋ ġlas;
Fiacha mac Eoġain ġan oil,
níor ṫreoruiġ a c-ceann Chairil.

[1] fá reaċ.   [3] a ġarriaḋ.

[2] *Cormac Cleireach*. Dr. O'Brien in his Irish Dictionary, under the word *Curmac*, calls him Cormac Mac Carthaigh, and says, that there was no other foundation for his being called *Royal Bishop of Munster*, than because he had repaired the Cathedral of Cashel, and two churches at Lismore, and was otherwise reputed a man of a pious and holy life. He refers to an ancient Irish MS. of the Four Gospels deposited in his time in the British Museum, written by *Mael Brighide*, in the margin of which a note appeared in the writer's hand, relative to the death of Cormac Mac Carthaigh, who, he says, was A.D. 1138, treacherously killed by *Diarmuid*

THE KINGS OF THE RACE OF EIBHEAR,

TRANSLATED BY MICHAEL KEARNEY, A.D., 1635.

1 Casshell the Citty was, of noble Mogha's Sonnes,
    Its spetious hewe soe flourished;
  From Corcke to Cormock Cleireaghe's Raignes,
    Their Kinges that Pallace well nourished.

2 And the family great from Oilill Oll that came,
    Eoghan Mor at Casshell sate not;
  For that prudent kinge for eloquence rare,
    That seate was not his lott.

3 And white-haired Kyan, and Cormac Cas,[1]
    That goodly seate did want;
  Which Ffiachae the son of Eoghuin failed,
    In that soyle to liue or plant.

Sugach O'Conchubhair Ciarraidhe; and he says that at the end of the book, the following note appeared also: *Oraid do Mhael-Brighte O'Mael Uanig qui scripsit hunc librum in Ardmacha is an bliain ro marbad Cormac Mac Carthaig Ri-Easpog Mumhan."* &c.

[1] *Cormac Cas*, the son of *Oilioll Olum*, and supreme king of Munster and Leinster, in the third century. He is the stock of the *Dal-Cassian* race, from whom descended the *O'Briens*, the *MacMahons of Thomond*, the *MacNamaras*, &c.—Vide *O'Brien's Irish Dictionary*.

Níor fan a (n) dá Oilioll ann,
dá mac Fiacha na n-óglann;
gíod mór gnaoi Caisiol do¹ cluin,
nocar faoi lairion Lugaid.²

Corc mac Luigdeac laocda [an] fear,
céad fear do cóirig Caiseal;³
fá muic do bí an baile,
go b-fuair é an dá mucaide.⁴

Mucaid ríog Múrgruige móir,
Dúrdaire [a] ainm níor eagcóir;
ar Ciolann tré péide riob,
mucaig ríog Eile uasail.

Ar iad fuair fát an baile,
ar t-tús a n-Druim Fiodbuide.
Druim Fiodbuide gan loch liob,
ionmuine le Corc Caisiol.

Do ronad banuis briogac,
dar tog Caisiol caoim-gníomac;
ag buime Chuirc Chairil cáig,
ro tairig Tuirc dá tógbáil.

Raitleann, ingean Dató tréin,
buime Chuirc Cairil caoim-péid;
trí céad muc, (is) trí céad mart,⁵
lucht an cuirig do coroig.

Do cuireað ran banais d'feoil,
trí láir an coire cóir-cóir;
sluaid nár tláit ríona mar roin
co n-a rait fiona Frangcaid.

¹ ró cluin.
² noc ar fris leo an ait rin.
³ céad fear do fuig a c-Caisiol.
⁴ aodaire.
⁵ trí céad mart, trí céad muc roir.

4 Both these Oiliolls brave, stoute Ffiachae's Sonnes,
　　Casshell was not their right Pallace;
　Nor for its ghesse did Lughuidh it take,
　　Fates from him kept that solace.

5 But Corck[1] his sonn, a valourous branch,
　　Did Casshell first entrance yield;
　By foggs concealed, till at last by chance,
　　Two swyne-heards found that field.

6 One Durdaire[2] called, the King of Muskry served,
　　And the other Kiolarne, from Eile kinge;
　These Swyne keepers two, there fatting their hoggs,
　　To our view this place did bringe.

7 To these two at first Druim Ffiodhbhuidhe was
　　Discovered, which Corcke did much affect;
　That soyle from faults more cleerly being,
　　His mind did it respect.

8 And for Ioy to gain that eminent place,
　　Corcke's nutrix largely feasted;
　And freely spent fatt porkes amaine,
　　Casshells's forts to frame well seated.

9 Raithlionn the Daughter of Datho the stronge,
　　Was Corcke Chaisshill's foster mother called;
　Three hundred beefes and hoggs as many,
　　Her cauldron to that feast well boyled.

10 And that furnace thrice with meate shee filled,
　　That feast to fitt with credditt;
　Of Shannayne the Lord of his Traine to please,
　　Ffrench wynes did raise her merritt.

---

[1] *Corc*, according to Mr. O'Flaherty was the grandson of *Oilioll Flannbeag*, by his son *Lughaidh*, the founder of the kings of Munster, and was the first who kept his court at Cashel. The place in which it was situated, was called *Corca Eathrach*, and extended in length from *Tibraid Fearainn*, now *Tiobraid Arainn*, (Tipperary,) near the Abbey of Holy Cross, to *Dun Andriais*, and the north side of Knockgraffon.—*Ogyg.* p. iii. c. 81.

[2] *Durdaire-Kiolarne*. Two herdsmen belonging to the kings of *Eile* and *Muscraidhe Thire*, who drove their herds to feed into the woods, were the first who discovered Cashel.—*Vide Keating,* p. 18, Dub. 1819. In *Leabhar na c-Ceart* they are called *Durdru* and *Cularan*.

Ó Mhaḋ Nuaḋaḋ¹ na c-céaḋ c-caṫ,²
ꜱo Dómnall O'm-briꜱan m-breaṫaċ;
cuirfioḋ ir rnaióm ḋoiliꜱ ḋíom,
ainm ar oiꜱiḋ ꜱaċ aird-ríoꜱ.

Eoꜱan Taiꜱleaċ na t-taoḃ reanꜱ,
beaꜱ naċ ar aird-ríoꜱ Eireann;
ḃár an Mhail³ a Maiꜱ Léna,
ḃaiḋ uile ár n-aird rꜱéala.

Do aireamuir, ní h-óráḋ raoḃ,
Macniaḋ, Conaire ceann-ċaoin;
ró ba rí Macniaḋ a muiꜱ,
rlat ꜱrian mín ir an Mhúmuin.

Trí riċiḋ bliaꜱain ꜱo h-oll,
ro ba rí Oilioll Olom;
ꜱo ruꜱ crine cruaiḋ ror ċraiḋ,
ní fuair ḋine dá ḋionꜱmail.

Ceaṫarċaḋ do Ċormac Car,
or iaṫ mór Muman mion-ꜱlar;
fuair ꜱan tlár aꜱ Súir rleaċtuiꜱ.
a ḃár a núir iꜱtleaċtuiꜱ.

Fiacha Muilleaṫan ꜱan meaṫ,
dá fiċiḋ eile ar éin leaṫ;
Leaṫ Cuiñ ró loir ar ró leaḋ,
ꜱur ċuit ran tuiñ [don] tairreal.

Móḋ Corb fiċiḋ bliaḋain ḃiñ,
Connaċtaiꜱ tuꜱ a ċuitim;
le mac ꜱaraiꜱ an taoiḃ ꜱil,
le h-Aoḋ do ċaḃuir Ċruaċuin.

¹ *Mogha Nuadhat*, is known in Irish history by the following names: *Eoghan Fidhfheathach*, *Eoghan Taighleach*, *Eoghan Mor*, and *Mogha Nuadhat*. He was called "*Na g-Cath*," from the various battles fought against the kings of Munster; but after giving battle to *Conn Cead-chathach* on the plains of Moylena, he was killed by *Goll Mac Morna* whilst asleep; and there are yet to be seen at this place two hills, in one of which it is said the corpse of *Eoghan Mor* was interred, and in the other that of *Fraoch*, a Spaniard, who was also slain there. *Conn*, after this engagement, was proclaimed monarch of Ireland.—*Ogyg.*, part iii. c. 60.

² c-creaṫ.

³ *Mal*, a king, prince, poet, soldier, or champion.—*O'Brien*.

11 From Mogha Nuadhadh of preyes that a 100 gott,
To Donnell O'Brien Iuditious;
Ffor name each kinge I will sett forth,
And his Death, bee it good or vitious.

12 Eoghan Taighleach fyne, by fame renowned,
The monarchy allmost mounted;
And by his violent Death on Lena field,
Our greatest newes were drowned.

13 Recount I might without mistake,
Macniad and Conaire free;
The first of Muighe was surely king,
Mounster's shyneing branch was hee.

14 Oileall Olom[1] raigned full 60 yeares,
Vnparalelled in all his deeds;
Till in his end decreipt by age,
Death cowardly him laide aside.

15 Cormac Cass iust raigned over Mounster Shyres,
Full 40 yeares vndaunted;
And by the River of Swyre[2] his quick conceipts,
Basely by Death were chaunted.

16 And Ffiachae thriving still, Muilleathan[3] nicknamed,
Hee 40 yeares succeeded,
And half Conn did foyle and pillage full oft,
Till at Tuinn him death surprized.

17 Mogha Corb[4] his raigne 20 yeares held out,
And the Conatians him oppressing;
Hugh, being the son of Garvidh cleane,
Him Cruachuinn to ayd did sting.

---

[1] *Oilioll Olum*, son of *Eoghan Mor*.—*O'Flaherty's Ogyg.* part iii. p. 225.

[2] *Swyre*. The river *Suir*, which takes its course by *Cahir, Newcastle, Clonmel, Carrick-on-Suir*, in the county Tipperary, and falls into the British Channel about five miles below Waterford.

[3] *Fiacha Muilleathan*, obtained the sovereignty of *Leath Mhogha*, after the death of his uncle, *Cormac Cas*, son of *Oilioll Olum*. He was treacherously slain by *Conla*, son of *Tadhg*, son of *Cian*, son of *Oilioll Olum*, at the ford called *Ath Uisiol*, upon the Suir.—See *Keating*, vol. i. pp. 403-4. Dub. 1809.

[4] *Mogha Corb*, son of *Cormac Cas*, King of Munster, aided by the *Fianna Finn* (Fionn's Irish militia,) slew *Cairbre Liffeachair* in the battle of *Gabbra Aicleidh*, but the celebrated militia were all cut to pieces, among whom fell *Oscar* and *MacLuigheach*, two renowned champions.—*Annals of Innisfallen*, A.D. 296.

Rug leam¹ Airgeat-Rois² na n-eac,
Oilioll Flann-mór³ na Muimneac;
fíce bliaġan buaiḋ gan béim,
fuair a riaraḋ g'á rí léim.

Oilioll Flann-beag, buaiḋ na breac,
tríocaḋ bliaġain ar ḋliġteac;
ḋár cuit faon ar fáta roll,
do ṫaċaḋ claon ran Chorain.

Eochaiḋ mac Oilolla féil,
aoin bliaġain déz³ go n-deiġ-méin;
go h-eaġ ran Múmain a muiġ,
fa puḋair an béḋ bunaiḋ.

Tríocaḋ bliaḋain do bí Coirc,
na ríġ Muman na mion port;
an téag ró ḋorcaḋ a ḋreac,
ró molbṫaḋ méaḋ na Muimneac

Naḋfraoic ba fiú fíce ríġ,
a ḋó 'ra deiċ gan di-mbríġ;
a ḃár cubaiḋ éġ do fuair,
fa béḋ ran Múmain mung-ruaiḋ.

Aongur mac Naḋfraoic ar cread,
ré bliaḋna déag ar fícead;
ḋár cuit rlat feartaċ⁴ nar ṫím,
Le mac Earca 'r le h-Oilill.

Eochaiḋ mac Aongura airḋ,
tríocaḋ bliaġan gan bioṫ mairġ;
uair ḋá raiḃe faoi dear zuil,
éġ na craoiḃe a g-cion Ċairoil.

¹ rug léim.

² *Airgead Rois*, where *Eireamhon* built his palace on the banks of the river Nore, within eight miles to the north of Kilkenny, and now known by the name of *Rathbeagh*.—Keating.

³ naoi m-bliaġana déag. ⁴ Flaiṫfearta.

18 Airgeadrois rich for horses being,
    Oileall Fflannmore¹ Ld Mounster ioy;
  Hee 20 yeares in a settled stay,
    Did raigne without annoy.

19 Oileall fflann-begg for Iudgement stoute,
    His raigne 30 yeares did stand,
  Till treacherously foyled at Coronn hee dyed,
    Distrust not deemeing at hand.

20 Eochuidh² the sonn of Oilioll free,
    19 yeares with praise hee raigned;
  His losse for griefe being a lasting sore,
    In Weast Mounster hee death sustained.

21 And 30 yeares over Mounster raigned,
    Corc their gratious Kinge;
  Till death his face obscurely left,
    And Momonians mindes did stinge.

22 Nadfraoich for fame worth 20 peeres,
    Hee 12 years raigned contynued;
  Ere his body and soule Divorced were,
    Which Mounster sadly ruined.

23 And Aongus the sonn of Nadfraoich³ raigned,
    Of yeares full 36;
  And confirmed in faith that Warriour to Death,
    Mac Earca and Oilioll did fix.

24 Noble Aonghus his sonn Eochuidh rightly called,
    Hee 30 yeares succeed;
  Who patient being, and prudently stoute,
    His life neere Casshell ended.

---

¹ *Oilioll Flann Mor*, son of *Criomhthan*, 134th monarch of Ireland. He was king of Munster, but leaving no heir, adopted his brother *Oilioll Flann Beag*, who was afterwards treacherously slain at *Coronn*, a district in the counties of Mayo and Sligo, and which it is said got its name from *Dian*, son of *Ceat*, of the *Danannian* race, who obtained it as a reward for his musical powers.—*Ogyg.* p. iii. cc. 69-81.

² *Eochaidh*, the son of *Oilioll Flann Beag*, had a great grandson called *Eugenius*, the father of six saints, who exhibited such shining virtues by their exemplary lives and miracles, that posterity canonized them as a just recompence for their pious lives. Their names are *Cormac*, *Becan*, of *Cill Beacain*, in Muskerry; *Calan of Gleanncaoin*, in *Ui-Lughaidh* in Munster; *Eibhin*, of *Ros-Mhic-Treoin*; *Diarmuid*, of *Cill Mac Eoguin*, in Carberry, and *Baothan* of *Cill Baothain*.—*Ogyg.* part iii, *ib.*

³ *Aongus Mac Nadfraoich*, was king of Munster, when St. Patrick en-

Crioṁċann ríċe bliaġain buan,
a c-Cairiol na c-colg rliom ruaġ;
mun ba h-éġ a oiġiḋ rin,
doiliġ ḟa ċéaḋ a cluinrin.

Triocaḋ bliaġain Cairbre Cruim,
ar nar iar áirḋ-rí uirruim;
ġeug bhanba noċar faġlaċ,¹
éġ rioġ Ġabra ir Ġleaṅ Aṁnaċ.

Feargur mac Criomċain na c-creaċ,
triocaḋ bliaġain fa buan breaṫ;
a éġ nior olc an diaċ ḋe,
ní Cliaċ, ar Crot, ar Claire.

Féilimiḋ mac Cairbre Cruim,
ċuiġ bliaġna ḋéaġ ḟa ḋeaġ ṁuirn;
do ḃé a oiġiḋ éġ an fir,
ġéġ Ċoḋail aġar Ċairil.

Éġ Fhinġin ṁic féil Aoḋa,
ṁic Criomċainn ċaiḋ creaċ laoċḋa,²
ġéaġ rioġḋa nar ona ċéaḋ³
trí bliaġna fiora fiċċeaḋ.

Ġabran a naoi ġo h-euġ ruair,
or Múṁain maġruiḋ ṁonġ ruaiḋ;
éġ beaċt an trealaṁ ġlain toir,
aġur⁴ Aṁalġaḋ uaroil

tered upon his mission, and was the first monarch converted to christianity. Keating, says, that when the saint was performing the rites of baptism, and on pronouncing the benediction over the king, who was standing, the point of the staff fell upon the king's foot, and penetrated it through, so that the blood flowed copiously from the wound; which, notwithstanding the great pain it caused, the king bore patiently, and from the great regard he had for the religion into which he was baptised he would not stir from the place till the solemn office was performed.

¹ ċaitleaċ.   ² laomḋa.

³ diamḋa CEAT.   ⁴ a reaċt.

25 And Criomhthan[1] his raigne being 20 good yeares,
 At Casshell hee life surrendred;
 Whose Death (if fates might alterred bee)
 More Ircksome was then a hundred.

26 To Monarch none submissiue being,
 Cairbre Cruimh raigned Thirty;
 Noble Bonavaes branch from spoyle most free,
 His death made Mounster heavy.

27 Ffearghus the sonn of Criomhthan that broyles,
 And battles fought with might;
 Hee fortunatly raigned full 30 yeares,
 And dyeing did Mounster fright.

28 Ffeilimidh[2] issueing from Cairbre Chruimh,
 15 yeares most happyly spedd;
 And naturall Death him takeing away,
 Sad griefe still Casshell fedd.

29 And Ffininn[3] the sonn of ffeill Aodha mild,
 Of Criomhthuin issueing stoute;
 This Regall branch in battle fierce,
 23 yeares raigne held out.

30 Nyne yeares over Mounster large,
 Raigned Garbhane ere hee dyed;
 In ffraigne parts, and next 7 yeares,
 Amhalghoidh him succeeded.

---

[1] *Criomhthann*, sat upon the throne of Ireland, A.D. 366, and was a man possessed of much princely accomplishments; but the intrigues of his sister, who prepared a dose of poison for him in order to obtain the crown for her own son, and which she found means to adminster, sealed his fate at *Sliabh Oighidh an Righ*, northward of Limerick.—*Keating*.

[3] *Feidhlimidh*, the son of *Cairbre*, was king of Desmond, A.D. 590; and was succeeded by *Gabhran* and *Amhalgaidh*, who reigned conjointly. *The Annals of Innisfallen*, record the death of *Amhalgaidh*, after having granted *Cluain Umha* (Cloyne, in the county of Cork) to God and St. Colman, A.D. 604. Under the same year is recorded the death of *Colman* son of *Leinin*, disciple of *Breannan*, abbot of Clonfert, and first bishop of Cloyne, in the south of Munster.

[4] *Finghin*, son of *Aodha Dubh*, (Black Hugh,) succeeded *Amhalgaidh* on the throne of Desmond, A.D. 604, and died, A.D. 619,—*Annals of Innisfallen*.

A cúig d'Aoda go h-eug a bur,
aon bliagain déag Cairbre c-cumur;
ég do mun ar ég fuigle,[1]
gég cró na g-céad g-cómairge.

Catal mac Aoda [a] éag réim,
adbar ríg Eireann eirém;
da deic ór Múmain maoinig,[2]
don cleic fagburg fanbfaoilid.[3]

A ceatair déag Failbe Flan,
ég mic Aoda na n-ór lan;
ba gníom learg ag báid ar cél,
gur mearg Chaig agar Cairél.

Mac Amalgaid éag do fuair,
deic m-bliagna do'n laoc cran ruaid;
a reacd déag don Mhuineac min,
ég do mac faobrac Fhinigin.

Cú gan Macair buan a blaid,
tri bliagna go bár c-Catail;
duine ar raic ór gac droing;
ad bác don bhuide Chonoill.[4]

Colga mac Failbe, flait fiall,
da bliagain gan ró dig-miad;
ég do fuiling[5] tocair toir,
a t-torcair a c-ceann Charoil.

A reacd déag ba buan an breat,
Fiongaine flait na Muimneac;
ég d'Ua Aoda na neac reang,
géig laomda ró creac Cuilleañ.

Eberrgeol raor, ré bliagna,
gníom mór éag an airid-iarlad;
mac Maolruadna[6] ba griod gai,
tug ann gac Dúnaig déarad!

[1] mar an éag roime. [2] maigrícc. [3] fubaicc faorfailge.

[4] *Buidhe Chonoill*, a plague which raged in Ireland, A.D. 665, and swept off a great portion of the population, making no distinction between age or sex, prince or peasant,—*Ogyg.* vol. 2, p. 408.

[5] éag d'Ua Floinn. [6] Maoil Uma.

31 Before his Death over Mounster king,
Fiue yeares to Hugh, were lent;
And by Cairbre in that power,
11 yeares more, with ioy were sweetely spent.

32 Cathall, the sonn of Hugh, lately named,
Ere death did him decline,
Hee 10 yeares raigned over Mounster all,
And Monarch (if hee liued) had beene.

33 Ffailbhe Fflann, his raigne 14 yeares held out,
Armed Hugh his hopefull sonn :
Interred in Earth, by his memory stormes,
At Cliadh and Caishell did come.

34 Cuain, nicknamed Chuainn Ruaidh, for fame,
15 yeares his raigne did hold;
And Maonach milde fierce Ffinnine his sonn.
14 years in life well told.

35 Long lasting Cathull motherlesse being
Three yeares hee raigned full,
His flourishing state did others exceede,
Till the plague his life did pull.

36 Colgha Ffailbhe his sonn, a giver free,
One yeare hee raigned not blemished;
And neare Casshell dyed that generous branch,
From the family of Fflann, derived.

37 Mounster's Soveraigne dear Ffionghuine called,
14 yeares[1] (a happy Chance)
Hughe's offspring raigned before hee dyed,
And Cuilleann left in a trance.

38 Edirsgel[2] free, six yeares hee raigned,
His death of peeres the sorest;
Maoil Vmha his sonn carrying his speare at will
Turned mansions with teares to forrests.

---

[1] Seventeen years in the corresponding Irish stanza.

[2] *Eidirsceoil*, son of *Eoghan*, king of Munster, was killed by *Nuadha Neacht*, of the Heremonians of Leinster, at *Aillinn*, and was declared monarch of Ireland; but he only enjoyed the sceptre six months when *Conaire* enquiring into the assassination of his father *Eidirsceoil*, retaliated on *Nuadha*, by killing him at the battle of *Cliach*, and from thence returning victorious, levied a fine on the people of Leinster for the murder of his father. The Lagenians, in conformity to a most solemn treaty and obligation, resigned for ever to the seven kings of Munster at

Cormac mac Oiliolla ruaiɴ,
ré bliaʒna déaʒ ʒo n-deaʒ-buaiḋ;
dear do bnaiṫ ʒanʒ na ʒaile,
tóin a c-cat Ạirḋ-Fheanʒaiḋe.

Bliaʒain aʒur triocaḋ triom,
mac Fioɴʒuiɴe na b-fóplaɴɴ;
Caṫal ʒéaʒ ɴáɴ tuʒaḋ toir,¹
puḋar a éaʒ mun am roiɴ.

Slat ċaoṁ ʒo n-oiɴbearc n-deiʒrceoil,
mac raoɴ oiḋṁic Eiḋinɴʒeoil;
a reaċt triocaḋ deiṁiɴ liom,
no ʒaḃ Caṫaraċ Cúil-fioɴɴ.

Maolḋuiɴ na m-bnaiʒḋeaɴ² m-breaʒḋa,
a ḋeiċ ra h-oċt oirneaʒḋa;
bneaʒ na maɴbna ní molfuiɴ,
eʒ aɴ Ạnɴaiʒ inʒeaɴ ċruiɴ.

Fiacha airḋ-ɴí ba h-úr drear,³
éaʒ d'Ua Chuirc o Chaɴɴ Luiḋeaċ;
a ceaṫair ḋéaʒ tnúṫʒal toin,
éʒ ba laṫṁun la Laiʒɴoiḃ.

A reaċt fiċeaḋ ba reiḋiṁ teaɴɴ,
Feiḋliṁ fiú flaiṫ Eineaɴɴ;
Ciarán⁴ mac aɴ t-raoiɴ ḋa ʒuiɴ,
ʒun ċuit ṫne aoiḃ na foluiʒ.

Cashell, that tract of Ossory, extending from *Gabhran*, (Gowran,) to *Grianan*, in the county Tipperary, as an atonement for the murder of this king, in the formal words of surrendering, "heaven and earth, sea and land, sun and moon."—*Ogyg.* p. iii, p.149, 150.

¹ ṫubaḋ foiɴ. ² n-Dúnaḋ.

³ Ạirt-ɴí ra h-úr drear,
fiċeaḋ bliaʒan re n-aiɴioṁ;
a h-oċt deaʒ deanḃ tnúṫʒal foiɴ,
éaʒ ra luṫṁan a Laiʒniḃ.

⁴ Ciarán Cluana nó earʒuiɴ,
ʒun ċuit (ʒioḋ ṫruaʒ) na falaiḋ.

39 Cormac (cold Oilliolla his sonn)
16 yeares raigne triumphed,
Till at Ard Arvidhe field hee killed was,
For chivalry him none surmounted.

40 Ffull 30 yeares space Mac Ffionghuine raigned,
Of Martialists full and vsefull;
And Cathal the sparke not settled in the East,
His death that time was dolefull.

41 Twenty eight[1] I knowe Cathusach Cuilfionn raigned,
A free branch old historyes likeing;
The sonn most milde for excellent feates
From Eidrisgeoil his Shyre deriving.

42 Maolduinn for feastes illustrious being,
18 years hee iustly raigned;
In his mourneing verses lett lyes surcease,
At Arnuidhe him death bereaved.

43 Ffiachae Airtre of spetious hue,
Of the progeny of Corck descending;
15 yeares[2] space in Norman's spight,
And of Leinster hee raigned while liveing.

44 Ffeilimidh,[3] fitt a Monarch to be,
Of Ireland all, to Twenty,
Adding 7 yeares over Mounster raigned,
Ere Kyaran him killed most basely.

---

[1] In the corresponding stanza I find 37 years as the period attributed to *Cathusach Cuilfhionn's* reign; this discrepancy of date occurs in several of the stanzas; I will not presume to make any alterations, but leave the reader to judge for himself, my object being to confine myself throughout to the text of my originals.

[2] Fourteen years in the corresponding stanza.

[3] *Feidhlimidh*, governed the province of Munster twenty seven years, and having entered into holy orders, presided in the Archiepiscopal chair of *Leath Mhogha*, as the south half of Ireland was generally called. His reign was marked by broils and contentions, but he always came off successful; but did not long survive to enjoy the benefit of his victories.— See *Keating*.

Dá chéad déag do ghléire Gall,   .i. Lochlannaicc.
do mairb Conchubar áir teann¹
cat Sgéit Neachtain gan clár toir,²
bár do cheartaig na chomoir.

A h-ocht Ailgeamoin na n-each,
go n-deachaig d'éag ar aoin leat;
Naolguala na Goill ior guin,
a h-ocht uada go ndoircuir.³

A trí déag do ir mín feidm,
Cionfaolaig mac Airc Thigearn;
ég da mathair da gné gil,
no gur folaig cré Cairil.

[A ceathair déag ir dearb leam,
Donchad mac Duib-Dá-bhoireann;*
fá béad a c-Cairiol na c-cnead,
d'éag do'n cat rin a c-Cairéal.]

A reacht do Dub-lachtna donn,
nó go n-deachaig d'éag obann;
bár Fionnguine fuair le real,
a ré Fionguine Feidlimig.⁴

Mac Cuilleanáin Cormac mín,
Airb-earpog agus Airb-rig;
a reacht nar loit gaoth na Goill,
gur thuit an laoch la Laignig.

At-bliagain reacd ní cealuib,
mac ioriugthteach Muinemen;
ég do Fhlaitbeartach na b-flead,
Flaitbeartach géag na c-clóideam.

¹ údmall.
² ceithre bliagana déag a éag fuair
géag laomda do chneach Craoib Ruaig.
³ a reacht uada go a atchoir.   ⁴ flathar.

* Donchad mhaic Dómnuill, mhaic Aoda, mhaic Ceanfaolad.

45 Next Ollchobhar¹ stronge over Norman's power,
    Twelue hundred of their forces killed;
  And Vndaunted being at Sgeith Neachthuyne field,
    There life hee bravely ended.

46 Ailghionan that kept great store of horses,
    8 yeares did his life affoord;
  And Mhaolghuala stiffe the Danes to smitt,
    One yeare² hee raigned with his sword.

47 Macthighearnae's sonn Keann-ffaola named,
    With power at Mayne hee raigned;
  13 yeares ere Death surprised his fame,
    And his Corps at Casshell layed.

48 [Fourteen years I do assert,
    Donagh the son of Dubh-dha-bhoirean reigned;
  Sorrowful news to Cashel of the conflicts,
    His death in the battle of Cashel.]

49 Dubhlachta na-Tonn from the waves soe called,
    For 7 yeares his raigne was bold;
  And suddaine Death him takeing away,
    Like yeares did Ffionghuine hold.

50 Mac Cuilionaine's³ sonn a Regall Bpp. being,
    Cormac milde his raigne iust lasted:
  Ffor 7 yeares space well filled with grace,
    Till in Leinster to death hee fasted.

51 Jonmhuinein his sonn hee Fflaithbheartach⁴ called,
    For stouting wise and wary;
  A giver free, for feastes well sett,
    For 13 yeares raigne did tarry.

---

¹ *Ollchobhar*, abbot of Imly, a man ambitious and fond of power, had interest sufficient to have himself elected king of Cashell, but was killed in the battle of *Sgiath Neachtain*.

² Eight years in the corresponding stanza.

³ *Cormac Mac Cuileannain*, lost his life by a fall from his horse at the battle of *Bealach Mughna*, fought against *Flann Sionna*, monarch of Ireland, aided by the forces of Leinster. For the particulars of this engagement, and a list of the slain at both sides.—see *Keating*, vol. 2, pp. 217-18-19. Mr. O'Flaherty says that his death occurred on a Tuesday, on the seventeenth of August, A.D. 908.—*Ogyg*. part iii. p. 561.

⁴ *Flaithbheartach Mac Ionmhuinion*, abbot of *Inis-Catha*, was taken prisoner at the battle of *Bealach Mughna*, and led in triumph among the other

bliaḋain ꝟo leiṫ Lorcán lonn,
nó ꝟo n-beaċaiḋ b'éaꝟ obann;
ꝟiolla laomḋa,¹ corp nár ċar,
Lorcán ꝟa ꝟraoċḋa loinꝟar.²

Ceallaċán, Cealla bo ḋíon,
cúiꝟ bliaḋain ḋo na Árb-ríḟ;
éaꝟ bo ḟéiꝟ ċaoiꝟean na tiḟ,
éaꝟ nár raoileaḋ an t-éaꝟ rin.

Maol Foċartuiḟ³ ꝟeaḋ a ré,
ceitre bliaḋna ꝟa buan ꝟné;
ꝟa béb rbuaiꝟ borboirneaċ bóir,⁴
rluaiꝟ Orruiḋeaċ bá ꝟaḋ ḃóḋ.⁵

A bó, Duiḃ-ba-ḃoirneaṁ ḋéin
ꝟur marḃ O'Liaċáin láin-ꝟéir;⁶
ba truaḟ an Cliaċár bá ċur,
rluaḟ O'Liaċáin bá leónaḋ.⁷

Fear ꝟraiḟ mac Áilꝟeannáin áirb,
bá bliaḋain bon cleiṫ coṁ-ꝟairꝟ;
rꝟéal bar milleaḋ bon ꝟréin ꝟil,⁸
a ċineaḋ ꝟéin ror ꝟoḋbaḋ.⁹

A ceaċair béaꝟ uair éiꝟin,
Maṫꝟaṁain mac Cinéibiḟ;
rꝟéal raoḃ-ṫruaḟ teaṁ an ꝟaċ toiḟ,
ꝟeall Maoilmuaiḋ ar an míliḋ.

Da bliaḋain bo Mhaoilmuaiḋ maiṫ,
tar éir ꝟill ar an ḃ-prim-ꝟlaiṫ;¹⁰
tá a ꝟ-caṫ Leaċta a leaċt,
aꝟur a ꝟeart an éinꝟeaċt.

A cúiꝟ¹¹ béaꝟ ꝟíra ċarla,
brian na Árb-ríoꝟ orꝟarḃa;
a ttorċar a c-Cluain Tarḃ toir,
aꝟur ꝟuair b'arm a oiꝟaiḟ,

captives by *Cearbhall*, king of Leinster. He was the author and fomenter

¹ maorḃa.   ² laomḋa lonꝟḃrar.   ³ Fóꝟartaċ
⁴ bonn-ḃreaċaċ mear.   ⁵ bo ró ċear.   ⁶ láin-réir.
⁷ leaḋraḋ.   ⁸ ꝟo n-ꝟréin n-ꝟlain.   ⁹ ꝟaꝟuiḃ.
¹⁰ tar éir a ꝟeaill ꝟo naiṫꝟear,
a ccaṫ bealaicc Leaċta a leaċt.
¹¹ a bo béaꝟ   a reaċt béaꝟ.

52 Warrlike Lorcann raigned 18 Monethes alone,
  Ere suddaine death him tooke:
With Sayles well manned hee stored was,
  And of body fair and stoute.

53 Ceallachan for the Church a prime defence,
  Hee Monarche's name enioyed;
Full 10 yeares space till a thunderbolt,
  His life vntimely annoyed.

54 Maolfotharthuighe's raigne 7 yeares did last,
  Good fortune still commaunding;
Till his pleasures to end the Ossorians wrought,
  Great griefe that his peeres did not kill him.

55 Dubh-Dha-Bhoirean fierce two yeares was king,
  Till Ld Liathaine's forces him killed;
With a Claster (him lost) of such a Traine,
  Full sad his friends still liued.

56 Both louely and tall Mac Ailghionan raigned 2 yeares,
  To his friends too short;
His death to the heart his kindred annoyed,
  And left them all *a-mort*.

57 In dangerous times Mahowne, Kenedye's sonn,
  14 yeares hee raigned iust;
In each house a cry Maolmhuaidh did raise,
  That basely him kill hee durst.

58 Proud Maolmuaidh raigned, that treachery donn,
  2 yeares without controule;
At Leachta-ffoord, is his heape of stones,
  And buryalls place in molde.

59 Brian,[1] Monarch was of Ireland all,
  12 yeares a powerfull warriour;
Till at Cluaintarbh field the Danes him killed,
  And his body buryed in Armo^E [Armoure]

of the broils which unhappily divided the two provinces at this time, and the cause of all the bloodshed on both sides; which circumstance enraged the clergy of Leinster, who prosecuted their resentment with that violence, that the unfortunate abbot was closely imprisoned and severely used, so long as *Cearbhall* lived; but after his decease he obtained his liberty.—*Keating.*

[1] *Brian Borumha*, monarch of Ireland, who, according to the Annals of Donegal, fell in the battle of Clontarf, in the eighty-eighth year of

* * * *
* * * *
* * * *
* * * *

Dar cloinn bud clann mairg go Cian,
 dan mairg ar Goill ar Gaillan;
 bliaġain do Dhonnċaḋ ar dearb leam,
 na Mhál ar móirleac Eireann.

An fear ceart do ċóiḋ ar ceal,
 ag teact o Róim na rig neaṁ;
 bliaġain agur ficċe fuair,
 Toirdealbaċ mic Taiḋg, triaṫ buain.

Ar mait corp O'Thail Teaṁra,
 ar t-toċd go h-áil oireaḋga;
 cúig bliaġna go a éag fuair,
 Diarmuid O'brian go m-beartbuaiḋ.

A cúig do Chormac iar roin,
 éag do bóir-flait clann Cairċaig;
 do labair O'brian na m-brat,
 a c-coṁ-flaitear re Cormac.

"Caoġad Donċaḋ ir dearb leam,
 na Mhál ar móir leaċ Eireann;
 a Chriċ ceart do ċóiḋ ar ceal,
 ar t-teact ón Róim na rig fear."

"Da bliaġain ir ficċe fuair,
 Toirdealbaċ mac Taiḋg, triaṫ buain;
 do ċaiṫ corp O Tail Teaṁra,
 gan loċd go h-áil oireaḋga."

his age, on a Good Friday; but Mr. O'Flaherty, places more reliance on the authority of Marianus Scotus' Scottish Chronicle, from which he gives the following extract: "Brian, king of Ireland, is killed on Good Friday, the twenty-third of April, his mind and thoughts wholly employed in heavenly pursuits:" and adds: "From all which concurrent circumstances, we are fully persuaded, that it happened in the year 1014, 23rd of April."

60 Maolsheachlinn Mac Donnell succeeding him,
 As monarch at Tarragh raigned;
Nyne yeares well spent, and omitted why?
 Let O'Dowgaine it shew, that failed.

61 "His children were children of sorrow except Cian,
 Their troubles were caused by the Galls and Galenians;
I have ascertained that Donchadh was one year,
 King of the largest half of Eire."

62 "The just man, whose spirit fled to Heaven, on leaving Rome,
 After preparing himself as king for the realms of glory,
Toirdhealbhach son of Tadhg, reigned
 One and twenty years without interruption."

63 "Great were the forces of O'Thail of Tara,
 They made a noble and magnificent display,
The victorious career of Domhnall O'Brian,
 Was five years to his death."

64 "Cormac, the chieftain of Clann Carthy,
 Reigned five years as his successor, (i. e. of Domhnall)
O'Brien of the garments claimed the sovereignty
 In conjunction with Cormac."

65 50 yeares, (good time,) did Donoghoe[1] raigne,
 Of halfe Modh all, being king;
His rightfull Lands Eclipsed were,
 While at Rome hee praiers did sing,

66 The powerfull peere Thorolagh Mac Teige[2] by name,
 Of O'Thail the prince at Tharragh;
Hee 12 years full as Monarch did sway,
 And to gaine it lead his Marrowe.

---

[1] *Donnchadh*, king of Munster, who undertook a pilgrimage to Rome, and died in the monastery of St. Stephens', where, it is said, his body is interred.

[2] *Toirdhealbhach*, the grandson of Brian Borumha, by his son *Tadhg*, who, after a tedious and lingering illness, died at *Ceann Coradh*, in the twenty-second year of his reign, and seventy-seventh of his age; the sixth of July, on a Tuesday, after having participated of all the rites of the Church.—*Ogyg.* part iii. p. 383.

" Tríocaḋ bliaḋain ḃaoi ós caċ,
    Muirċeartaċ mór na maol paċ;
    sgéal ḋar ġaḃaḋ Fionn-ṁaġ Foll,
    do ġalar iongnaḋ oḃaṅ."

" Cheiṫre bliaḋna go éag ruair,
    Diarmuid O' ḃriain na m-breaċ buaiḋ;
    a cúig déag Cormac ann sin,
    éag do ḃórr-ḟlait clann c-Cárrṫaiġ."

" Conċuḃar O'ḃriain na m-brat,
    a c-cóṁ-ḟlaiṫeas ré Cormac;
    éag ḟlaṫa cé is fóid aḋar,
    ré ḋá cúig do Ċonċúḃar."

" Taḋg mac Cárrṫa nár ċleaċt goiḋ,
    Toirḋealḃaċ O'ḃriain ḃárr-loiġ;
    éag na m-ḃeaċaiḋ tré ṁaiṫear,
    a ceaṫair a c-cóṁ-ḟlaiṫear."

" Chúig bliaḋna Muirċeartaċ mór,
    go n-ḋeaċaiḋ ḋ'éag gan tintóḋ;
    a cúig gan ḃéaḋ fórlaṅ fear,
    go h-éag Ḋoṁnaill fá ḋeireaḋ."

" Naoi ḃ-fir ḋéag don ḋréim ḋuarais,
    ḃuiliġ, breaġa, ḃiṫ-nuarair;
    nár loit um Cheallaiḃ a cáin,
    do ċuit do reaṅaiḃ ruaḋ-ġnaiċ."

" Móir-ṡeisear, ceaṫarċatt cóis,[1]
    ḋá n-aird-ríoġaiḃ ní h-eaḋóiġ;
    nár ḋirg agus nár ḋoċt teaġ,
    rug Corp Chríosd agus Creideaṁ."

" Noċ ar ġaḃ Aird-ríġ aṁlaiḋ,
    tar éis Ḋoṁnaill donn-ḟaḃraicc;
    Múṁain m-braonaicc t-toṁṫaicc, t-truim,
    c-coċlaicc, c-craoḃaicc, c-cleaṫ-ċuir."

[1] Seisear ar ċaegaḋ go cóir.

67 " Muircheartach[1] the Great of the broad-topped raths,
Reigned thirty years over his people,
It is related that fair Moy Fail was visited during his reign,
By a strange sickness that caused sudden deaths."

68 40 yeares successe with judgem^t sound,
To Diermott O'Brien, and Cormac,
Fiue years held out, who lofty was,
Till then him life forsooke.

69 And Conno^r O'Brien with Cormac joined,
In soveraignty held tenn yeares;
Off his ffather's soyle, its peere then fell,
Surviveing Connor appeares.

70 " Tadhg Mac Carthy, who practised warlike feats,
And Toirdhealbhach O'Brien, a sovereign prince;—
Two who spent their lives in deeds of benignity—
Reigned conjointly four years."

71 Ffiue yeares great Mortagh spent,
Ere life bade him adiewe;
And 5 times 5 of yeares oppressed,
That Donell did last its true.

72 " Nineteen princes of a worthy race,
Warlike, comely, and vigorous,
Who never failed to maintain the church,
Fell in the gory path of battle."

73 " Seven,—being eminently just,—
Of those great kings, without a doubt,
Who neither feared nor avoided death,
Received the blessed Viaticum, and died penitent."

74 " And they likewise, reigned kings supreme,
After Domhnall of the brown eye-brows,
Over Munster of the streams, of the rich rough crops,
And of the boughs drooping with loads of mellow fruit."

---

[1] *Muircheartach Mor*, king of Ireland, was the son of his predecessor, *Toirdhealbhach*; a short time before his death, he passed the residue of his days at Lios Mor, in all the rigours of christian abnegation.—*Vide Ogyg.* part 3, p. 385.

" Cuid ar mó do mín Éireann,
    iac Múman na mín-ṡléibeann;
    ar méid a h-uaisle 'sa h-óir,
    sa réad uaisri g'a h-onóir."

" Ar a c-cróḋacṫ ní ċelam,
    ní fríṫ orra aon éalang;
    an ḟaoire, an ḋealb-ġlaine a n-ḋreaċ,
    an meanamnaiḋe na Muimneaċ."

" Ar ċruaḋar a c-caṫ sé c-cleaċtaḋ,
    an tóirċuiḋe, an ṫoirbeartaḋ;
    an nór deaġaiṫne, séiḋ ruinn,
    an méinn sean-aiṫreaḋ réaġuin."

" Ar faisringe a t-tíre ḋe,
    ar a m-beiṫ ós cáċ coiḋċe;
    ar béin-reabraḋ fíṅ-fóid breaġ,¹
    ar ċleaṫ-ṡileaḋ a c-craoireaċ."

" Da ṫír ar aille an Éiriṅ,
    ḋa ċúige an Chlair léiḃiṅ;
    ṫír fóid-ḟeang aird-mín na n-gleann,
    Cóigeaḋ í d'Aird-ríġ Éireaṅ."

" O'Duḃaġain sean réim,
    feiċeaḋ mac Aisluinn eiréin
    Paittraicc sorarḋa na b-ḟear,
    ar Cómarba do Chaireal."

" Diarmuid Mhac Caṁċa chear geal,
    ar Ríġ ṫre ċóir ar Chaireal;
    bor ċaoiṁ-ḟeang do ċleaċt ġal,
    teaċt an sailġean coirreagta."*

C-A-I-S-E-A-L.

¹ ar méinn re féinn Fhinn na c-creaċ.

* teaċt an faoilean go ruca.

75   " The most important part of pleasant Eire,
Is Munster of the mountain-studded plains,
On account of her nobility, her wealth,
Her store of precious stones, and the honor her people support."

76   " I cannot conceal the good qualities of the men of Munster.
In whom no flaw was ever found ;
They were famed for love of freedom, comeliness of countenance,
And loftiness of spirit."

77   " They were inured to war at all times,
They were hospitable and liberal;
Their habits were calculaled to win confidence,
Being in strict conformity with those of their ancestors."

78   " Munster was also celebrated for the extent of her territory,
For the superiority of her women above those of other provinces,
As well in the melody and cheerfulness of voice, and charming features,
As in the excellent arrangement of their dress."

79   " The two Munsters of the undulating plains,
Are the most delightful provinces of Eire. ;
A country of fertile glebe, of well-sheltered dales,—
'Tis a province befitting the monarch of Eire."

80   " O'Dubhagan, the aged and mild,
A vigilant follower of Mac Alpruinn, i. e.
Saint Patrick, exalted above all men,
Whose vicarage is Cashel."

81   " Diarmuid Mac Carthy of the fair skin,
The slender-framed man accustomed to valorous feats ;
Is rightful king of Cashel,
And blessed is the accession of him born on the sea."

C-A-S-S-H-E-L.

COMMENTARY ON
'THE KINGS OF THE RACE OF EIBHEAR'

In the following Commentary the verse number precedes the line enumeration. Historical Kings of Munster, as opposed to semi-mythological ones, are cross referenced against their order of succession as enumerated in Appendix One, and in the genealogical charts in Appendix Two, by the reference cited immediately after their personal names; for example COIRPRE CROMM [6] was the sixth King of Cashel.

1:1. 'Mogha,' or, more properly, Leth Moga, is an archaic term used to describe that half of Ireland lying south of an imaginary line drawn between Dublin in the East and Galway in the West. According to the early medieval synthetic historians Conn Cáthcatach (Conn of the Hundred Battles), ancestor of the Uí Néill and Uí Briúin dynasties, and Mug Nuadat ('the slave of the god Nuadu'), ancestor of the Eóghanacta of Munster, semi-mythological kings of the mid second century A.D., divided the island into 'Leth Cuinn,' or Conn's Half, and Leth Moga, 'the Slave's Half.' Professor Byrne has stated that: "Names compounded of the element and a divine name are frequent in the prehistoric pedigrees of the south of Ireland...but they disappear in the Christian period. The same concept however persists in names compounded with 'tonsured, devotee,' 'client, vassal' and Gilla 'servant' prefixed to the names of Saints ..." (Byrne, F.J., 'Irish Kings and High-Kings,' London 1973, page 168).

1:3. 'Corcke,' otherwise Conall Corc [1] established Cashel as the seat of the Eóghanacht Kings in the late fourth century of the Christian era (see Commentary note 5:1). The last of his descendants to reign therefrom was 'Cormock Cléireagh' ('Cormac the Cleric') better known to history as the King-Bishop Cormac III MacCarthy [46d] (see Commentary note 64:1.). Cormac's exact ecclesiastical status is uncertain but there can be little doubt that he was a monk. In 1127, following his deposition by the nobility of Munster, Cormac sought refuge in the great monastery at Lismore, County Waterford, and "took the tonsure there" (Ó hInnse, Seamus., 'MacCarthaigh's Book,' in *Miscellaneous Irish Annals*,' Dublin 1947, page 19). There are several contemporary references to Cormac which refer to him as Rigepiscop or 'Bishop-King' and he is so described in an obituary notice in the Annals of Loch Cé: "1138: Cormac, son of MacCarthaigh, chief King of Desmumha, and Bishop-King of Erinn in his time as regards piety, and presentation of jewels and valuables to clerics and churches, and ecclesiastical riches, in books and utensils to God... fell in treachery by the people of Taudh-Mumha; and a blessing be on his soul"

Despite such references it is unlikely that Cormac was consecrated as a Bishop during his brief exile at Lismore. Had he been, one would certainly expect to find some reference to the fact in Saint Bernard of Clairvaux's 'LIFE OF SAINT MALACHY' which refers to the King at length. All that one can deduce from that source is that during the time of his forced exile at Lismore Cormac wished to be regarded as "one of the poor brethren," which is to say as a monk, although there is no specific reference to him having received the tonsure:

> Whilst the Bishop (of Lismore) was getting ready to receive (King Cormac) with the honour due to him, he turned it down, remarking that he was willing to be considered as one of those poor brethren who were his companions. He preferred to lay aside his royal pomp and be content with common poverty, to look forward to God's will rather than recoup his kingdom by force. Nor did he wish to shed blood which would cry out to God from the earth against him. The Bishop rejoiced at hearing this. Astonished at his devotion, he granted his wish. What more should I say? To the King was given a poor little hut to live in and Malachy for his teacher, bread with salt and water for food. The very presence of Malachy served as the King's sweetmeats. (Meyer, R.T., ed. 'The Life and Death of St. Malachy the Irishman,' Michigan 1978, p. 25).

Even the explicit reference in *MacCarthaigh's Book* to Cormac receiving the tonsure must be treated with some caution as it is a mid-fifteenth-century recension of earlier annals and is not therefore contemporary with the reign in question. *The Annals of Inisfallen*, which are, merely state that:

> Cormac son of Mac Carthaig, King of Desmumu, was deposed by the men of Munster themselves, and he entered Lismore. (entry sub: 1127)

It would be tenuous, to say the least, to argue that "entered Lismore" is to be understood as a reference to Cormac entering Holy Orders.

Given the uncertainty concerning his exact canonical status it is probable that the title 'Bishop-King' arose in consequence of Cormac reviving the Eóghanacht coronation rite, almost certainly abandoned by the Dál gCais usurpers, wherein the king was anointed and received 'Holy Orders' (MacCarthy Mór, The., 'Historical Essays on the Kingdom of Munster,' Kansas City, MO 1994, pages 1 - 18). The ninth-century VITA TRIPARTITA refers to the fact that the Kings of Munster were 'ordained' by the *comarba* of Saint Patrick and thus "ruled under a crozier" (Byrne, F.J., 'Irish Kings and High-Kings,' London 1973, page 190, citing VITA TRIPARTITA).

The Kings of the Race of Eibhear

2:1. 'Oilill Oll,' otherwise Ailill Olómm, King of Munster, was the son of Mug Nuadat (alias Eóghan Mór, alias Eóghan Taidlech). He reigned in the mid third century. According to GENEALOGIE DE LA ROYALE ET SERENISSIME MAISON DE MacCARTHY, folio 4, he died in A.D. 260.

2:2. Eóghan Mór, II, son of Ailill Olómm by his wife Saba, daughter of Conn Céadchathach (Conn of the Hundred Battles), was the progenitor of the Eóghanachta Septs.

3:1. 'Kyan,' otherwise Cian, was the younger son of Ailill Olómm and the supposed ancestor of the O'Carrolls, O'Harras and O'Garras. Cormac Cass, his brother, was the spurious ancestor of the Dál gCais septs. Describing the usurpation of the throne of Munster by the O'Briens of Thomond in the late tenth century Professor F.J. Byrne has commented:

> Pedigrees were often remodelled for political ends. Perhaps the most blatant example is the fiction that the Dál gCais, rulers of a petty state in east Clare, were a collateral branch of the Eóghanacht, entitled from remote antiquity to share in the over-kingship of Munster. So deeply rooted were the claims of aristocratic descent that the spectacular rise to power of Brian Bóruma, and the consolidation of that power by the O'Briens, were not sufficient to promote the Dál gCais in the political hierarchy without the spurious lustre of ancestral prestige. ('Irish Kings & High-Kings,' London 1973, p. 11).

3:3. 'Ffiache,' more properly Fiachu Mullethan, son of Eóghan Mór, II. He is said to have been murdered in A.D. 270 by his first cousin, Conla, son of Cian (see Commentary note 3:1. above) whilst bathing in the river Suir (GENEALOGIE, folio 5).

4:1. According to the early medieval genealogists Fiachu Mullethan left issue, two sons, namely Olioll Flann Mór, otherwise Ailill Fland Mór, and Olioll Flann Beg, otherwise Ailill Fland Bec. The former died in A.D. 313, the latter in A.D. 343 (GENEALOGIE, folio 6).

5:1. 'Corck,' otherwise Conall Corc [1] alias Conall mac Luigtech, son of Luigtech and grandson of Ailill Fland Bec, is generally accounted the first historical as opposed to semi-mythological king of Munster. He established Cashel as the seat of the Eóghanacht dynasty. Later genealogists made him the ancestor not only of the several Eóghanacht septs but even of the so called 'Eóghanacht of Mag Geirginn' (or Mearns), the Lennoxes, and even the Stuarts of Scotland (Op.cit. Byrne, p. 194).

6:1. There are several 'finding legends' relating the 'discovery' of Cashel by Duirdriu and Cuirirán, swineheards employed by the kings of Éile and Múscraige (see: Dillon, Myles, ed. 'The Book of Rights,' Dublin 1984, page 3). They all preserve archaic references to the fact that, prior to the coming of Christianity, Cashel was not only the seat of the Kings of Munster but a Druidic cult centre (op.cit., MacKillop, *A Dictionary of Celtic Mythology*, page 92, and op.cit., Byrne, F.J., *Irish Kings & High-Kings*, pages 184 - 187).

7:1. Cashel was also known as Drumfeera, from the extensive woods surrounding it in the fifth century. Corc's settlement was known as 'Lis-na-laochru' or the 'fort of heroes' (Finn, Andrew., 'Royal and Saintly Cashel,' Dublin 1929, page 4) an undoubted reference to the Niadh Nask or Knights of the Golden Chain who served as the bodyguard of the Eóghanacht kings and who were often referred to as 'The Heroes of the Round Hill of Cashel.'

9:1. Corc's foster mother is elsewhere named Fedelma, a witch or fairy who, whilst casting a spell, accidentally burnt his ear. In early Irish 'corc' was glossed as 'crimson' or 'red' (MacKillop, James., *Dictionary of Celtic Mythology*, Oxford, 1998, p. 183). The earliest extant version of this story dates to the eighth century:

> Fedelma the witch, daughter of Móethaire of the Corco Óchae, was the fostermother of Conall Corc mac Luighthig. On the night that Corc was born the witch spent the night in the house of King Luighthech. His mother was Bolce Benbretnach of the Britons. She was a female satarist. On the king she put an irrefusable request that she should sleep with him. In consequence Conall mac Luigthig was conceived. The name of his fostermother, however, was Láir Derg ('Red Mare,' apparently a nickname of Fedelma's). Hence was called 'Corc mac Láire,' and hence too the Uí Maic Láire are so called.
>
> The witch was harrying the king in Femen where is Fertai Chonaill (the grave mounds of Conall). When his mother was delivered of Corc she put her son under the protection of Fedelma the witch, and on that account it is she who reared him.
>
> On the next day a coven was due. She concealed the boy under the hearth beneath the ground. The witches came into the house. One of them said: "I do not destroy except what is under the cauldron.' The fire darted at the child and burned his ear. As a result Corc mac Luighthig was red (corc) . . . (Hull, Vernam., in *Proceedings of the Modern Language Association*, LXII (1947)

9:4. These references to a magical feast, and cauldron, ultimately derive from the 'Cauldron of Abundance' possessed by the Dagda, or 'Good god' of the ancient Irish (Green, Miranda J., *Dictionary of Celtic Myth & Legend*, London 1992, page 58). Dagda was frequently represented as a stag headed divinity and in all probability the adoption of a stag as the clan

12:1. 'Eóghan Taigleach,' more properly Eóghan Taidlech was, of course, also known as Mug Nuadat and Eóghan Mór.

12:4. The Reverend Geoffrey Keating (1580 - 1650) states that Mug Nuadat was "treacherously slain by Conn Céadchathach (Conn of the Hundred Battles) who . . . killed him in his bed, in the morning of the day when they intended to fight the battle of Miagh Leane (Keating, The Rev. Geoffrey., *A General History of Ireland*, ed. Dermot O'Connor, Dublin 1861, page 247). Miagh Leane is coextensive with the modern village of Kilbride, near Tullamore, County Offaly (op.cit., MacKillop, page 167).

16:1. 'Ffiachae,' i.e. Fiachu Mullethan (see Commentary note 4:1).

16:3. 'Conn,' or rather Cormac mac Airt, King of Leth Cuinn, was defeated by Fiachu in battle and forced to surrender hostages, which is to say to admit the hegemony of Leth Moga:

> The valiant Fiachu Mullethan,
> The warlike monarch of the southern coasts,
> Received the hostages who came to from Tara,
> To Rathfuin and Rath Naoi (Op.cit., Keating, page 273)

16:4. Fiachu Mullethan was murdered in A.D. 270 by his cousin Conla, son of Tadhg, son of Cian (see Commentary note 3:1.) at Aith Uisiol on the river Suir (op.cit., Keating, page 279).

17:1. Mogha Corb, supposedly a son of Cormac Cass (see Commentary note 3:1), a semi-mythical King of Munster, is said to have been slain in A.D. 297 by Áodh, King of Connacht (op.cit., GENEALOGIE, folio 6).

18:2. 'Oileall fflannmore,' otherwise Ailill Flann Mór was according to all other authorities the eldest son of Fiachu Mullethan (see Commentary note 4:1). He supposedly died in A.D. 313.

19:1. 'Oileall fflan-begg,' otherwise Ailill Flann Bec, died in A.D. 343 (Op. cit., GENEALOGIE, folio 6).

20:1. 'Eochuidh' does not occur in Professor Byrne's list of the Kings of Munster. However the GENEALOGIE lists an 'Eochy,' King of Munster and identifies him as the son and immediate successor of Ailill Flann Bec.

21:2. Corc, otherwise Conall Corc [1]. He died before A.D 379 (Op.cit., GENEALOGIE, folio 8). Some authorities place his death after A.D. 438 claiming that he was one of the three kings who laboured with Saint Patrick to reconcile the Brehon Law with Christianity.

22:1. 'Nadfraoich,' more properly Nad Froích [2], son of Conall Corc. His name literally means 'bathed in wine' and refers to the legend that his mother, Aímend, bathed him in wine at birth to denote his royal status (Op.cit., Byrne, page 193). His father, Corc [1], prophesied that Cashel would be Nad Froích's city and that his descendants would reign from there as Kings of Munster:

> It will be Nad Froích's city;
> everyone's land will be Nad Froích's;
> he to whom Cashel belongs,
> all Munster will be in vassalage to him.
> (Op.cit., Byrne, page 196, citing a ninth-century text).

24:1. 'Aonghus,' or rather Óengus Mac Nad Froích [3], King of Munster, was supposedly baptised by Saint Patrick in A.D. 448. According to the ninth century VITA TRIPARTITA during the ceremony the Saint accidentally pierced the King's foot with his crozier. Óengus, believing this to be an essential part of the rite, made no complaint. Patrick, on discovering what had occurred is said to have blessed the King and promised him that neither he, nor any of his successors, would die a violent death. The subsequent history of the dynasty gives the lie to the legend. Following his baptism Óengus founded a Church on the Rock of Cashel which was served by two bishops, ten priests and seventy-two other religious (GENEALOGIE, folio 10). Óengus was slain at the battle of Cenn Losnada in A.D. 492 (*Annals of Inisfallen*).

24:1. 'Eochuidh,' otherwise Eochaidh [4] succeeded his father, Óengus Mac Nad Froích [3], as King of Munster. He may have reigned jointly with his brothers Dub Gilcach [4a] and Feidlimid [4b] (Op.cit., Byrne, page 291). Eochaidh died in A.D. 523 (Genealogie, folio 11).

25:1. 'Criomhthan' or Crimthann Srem [5], otherwise known as Crimthann Feimin, King of Munster, was the ancestor of the Eóghanacht Glendamnach. He is not to be confused with his brother Crimthann Airthir Chliach, ancestor of the Eóghanacht Airthir Chliach. Crimthann Srem was slain in A.D. 551 at the battle of Feimhim by Colman Bec, son of Diarmait mac Cerbaill, King of Leth Cuinn (died A.D. 565).

26:2. 'Cairbre Cruimh,' more usually written Coirpre Cromm [6], son of Crimthann Srem [5], died in A.D. 580 (*Annals of Inisfallen*).

27:1. 'Ffearghus,' otherwise known as Fergus Scandal [7], son of Crimthann Airthir Chilach, died in A.D. 583 (op.cit., Byrne, page 293) after a reign of three years rather than the thirty ascribed here.

28:1. Fergus Scandal [7] was succeeded as King of Munster by Feidlimid [8], son of Coipre Crom [6]. He died in A.D. 590 (op.cit., GENEALOGIE, folio 12; & *Annals of Ulster*) or A.D. 592 (*Annals of Inisfallen*). Accordingly he reigned for less than a decade rather than the fifteen years ascribed to him by our poet. Associated with him, possibly as co-kings or in some quasi viceregal capacity, were the brothers Amalgaid [8b] and Gárban

[8c]. They were the sons of Éndae, son of Crimthann, son of Ailill, son of Óengus Mac Nad Froích [3], King of Munster.

29:1. 'Ffininn,' actually Fíngen [9], son of Áed Dub, grandson of Crimthann, and great grandson of Feidlimid [4b], King of Munster, son of Óengus Mac Nad Froích [3] (see Commentary note 24:1). He attended the Council of Dromceat, A.D. 590, and died in A.D. 619 (*Annals of Inisfallen*) having reigned for 29 rather than 23 years. His reign was regarded as a golden age of prosperity. The *Annals of Tigernach*, noting his death, relate:

> Munster,
> in the time of Fíngen mac Áedo
> its store-houses were full,
> its homesteads were fruitful.

The fruitfulness of the land was of course considered a proof of the king's legitimacy as ruler. No kingdom could flourish under a usurper.

30:2. 'Garbhane,' otherwise Gárban [8c]. Little is known of this king saving that he reigned with, or succeeded his brother Amalgaid [8b] (Op.cit., Byrne, page 293).

30:4. 'Amhalghoid,' or Amalgaid [8b], elder brother of Gárban [8c], and apparently King of Munster in succession to Feidlimid [8a] (see Commentary note 28:1; and Op.cit., Byrne, page 293). His death is not recorded in the *Annals of Inisfallen* despite Mr. Daly's assertion to the contrary.

31:2. 'Hugh,' otherwise Áed Bennán [9a], King of Munster, descended from the sept of Eóghanacht Locha Léin. He died in A.D. 619 (*Annals of Ulster*) or A.D. 621 (*Annals of Inisfallen*).

32:1. Cathal [10], son of Áed Fland Cathrach and grandson of King Coirpre Cromm [6] (see Commentary note 26:2.). He died in A.D. 628.

33:1. Ffailbhe Fflann, otherwise Faílbe Fland [11], King of Munster, succeeded to the throne of Cashel in A.D. 628. He was a brother of Fíngen, King of Munster [9] (see Commentary note 29:1) and died in A.D. 637 (*Annals of Ulster*) or 639 (*Annals of Inisfallen*).

34:1. 'Cuain,' otherwise Cúán [12], son of Amalgaid [8b] (see Commentary note 30:4.) succeeded his kinsman Faílbe Fland [11] as King of Munster. He died in A.D. 641 (op.cit., Byrne, page 293) after a reign of 4 rather than 15 years.

34:3. 'Maonach,' or rather Máenach [13] was the son of Fíngen [9], King of Munster (see Commentary note 29:1.). He died in A.D. 662 (*Annals of Inisfallen; Annals of Ulster*) and was succeeded by his kinsman Cathal Cú-cen-máthair [14].

35:1. Cathul, otherwise Cathal Cú-cen-máthair [14] 'the motherless hound,' son of Cathal [10], King of Munster (see Commentary note 32:1.). He died in A.D. 665 (*Annals of Ulster*) or A.D. 666 (*Annals of Inisfallen*) of the plague (op.cit., Byrne 179).

36:1. 'Colgha Ffailbhe,' otherwise Colgú [15], was the son of Faílbe Fland [11], King of Munster (see Commentary note 33:1.). He succeeded to the throne in A.D. 665/666 on the death of his kinsman Cathal Cú-cen-máthair [14]. He died in A.D. 678 (*Annals of Inisfallen*) or A.D. 679 (*Annals of Ulster*).

37:1. 'Ffionghuine,' more properly Fínguine [16], King of Munster, was a son of Cathal Cú-cen-máthair [14] (see Commentary note 35:1.). He died in A.D. 695 (*Annals of Inisfallen*) or A.D. 696 (*Annals of Ulster*).

37:3. 'Hugh,' otherwise Áed Fland Cathrach (see Commentary note 32:1.), the great grandfather of Fínguine, and son of King Coirpre Cromm [6] (see Commentary note 26:2).

38:1. 'Edirsgel,' otherwise Eterscél [17], King of Munster, was the son of Máel Umai, and grandson of Cúán [12], King of Munster (see Commentary note 34:1.). He died in A.D. 721 (*Annals of Inisfallen*). The footnote to the poem is in error in stating that Eterscél was the son of a 'King Eóghan.'

38:3. Maoil Vhma, otherwise Máel Umai, father of Eterscél.

39:1. Cormac [18] succeeded his cousin Eterscél [17] as King of Munster in A.D. 721. His father, Ailill, was the son of Máenach [13], King of Munster, who died in A.D. 662 (see Commentary note 34:3.). The *Annals of Inisfallen* place his death in A.D. 713: "The battle of Carn Feradaig, in which Cormac son of Máenach, King of Cashel, fell."

40:1. 'Mac Ffionghuine,' otherwise known as Cathal Mac Fínguine [19], King of Munster, succeeded to the throne of Cashel in A.D. 713. He was the son of Fínguine [16], King of Munster who died in A.D. 695/696 (see Commentary note 37:1.). The *Annals of Inisfallen* report that he defeated the Kings of Leinster and Ossory at the battle of Feil in A.D. 735. Throughout his reign he strived to make a reality of Eóghanacht hegemony over Leth Moga, and with some success. In a poem entitled "Teist Cathail meic Finguine," preserved in the Book of Leinster, Cathal is styled "King of Munster, King of Connacht, High-King of Tara, King of Airgialla, King of the Deisi, King of Thomond, King of Aine and High-King of Ireland." His generosity to poets was legendary and guaranteed their reciprocal appreciation:

> The people who praised Cathucan,
> from the time that they entered his country
> until the time they left his assembly,
> were treated as kings by the High-King.
> (Op.cit., Byrne, page 210, citing a tenth-century poem)

Cathal mac Fínguine died in A.D. 742. Cathal son of Fínguine, King of Ireland, dies, of whom Mór Muman has said:

> In tImlech (Emly)
> Which Ailbe has ennobled by his crozier,
> One thing famous about it is
> Its earth covering the brow of Cathal.
> (*Annals of Inisfallen*)

41:1. For 'Cathusach Cuilfionn' read Cathussach [20], King of Munster. He was the son of Eterscél [17] (see Commentary note 38:1.) and great grandson of Cúán [12] (see Commentary note 34:1.).

42:1. 'Maolduinn,' otherwise Máel Duin [20a], King of Munster, was the great great grandson of Áed Bennán [9a], King of Munster, who died in A.D. 619/621. Máel Duin died in A.D. 786 (*Annals of Inisfallen*). He was succeeded by an Uí Fidgeinti, Olchobar [20b], Abbot of Innse Cathaig, who died in A.D. 796/7 (*Annals of Inisfallen*).

43:1. 'Ffiachae Airtre,' more commonly known as Artrí [21], King of Munster, was the son of Cathal Mac Fínguine [19], (see Commentary note 40:1.). During his reign the Norsemen began their raids on Ireland. He died in A.D. 821 (*Annals of Inisfallen*). Professor Byrne indicates that Artrí's son, Tuathal [21a], either reigned simultaneously with his father, or briefly succeeded him on the throne (op.cit., Byrne, p. 293). Artri/Tuathal were in turn succeeded by Tnúthgal [22], son of Donngus. The poet seems ignorant of the reigns of Tuathal and Tnúthgal.

The earliest known reference to the anointing of a Gaelic king at his accession relates to Artrí:

> The Law of (St.) Ailbe was proclaimed over Munster and the ordaining of Artrí, son of Cathal, to the Kingship of Munster.
> (*Annals of Inisfallen*, A.D. 793).

From this reference is is evident that Artrí was anointed by the Metropolitan of Munster, the Bishop of Emly. Emly was the See of Saint Ailbe, possibly a pre-Patrician Saint, and its primacy (the 'law of Ailbe'), rather than that of Uí Néill Armagh, was generally upheld by the Eóghanachta (see Commentary note 80:4).

44:1. 'Ffeilimidh,' otherwise Feidlimid IV mac Crimthainn, King of Munster [23], was the greatest Eóghanacht sovereign of the ninth century. There is no firm evidence to indicate that he was a Bishop let alone an Archbishop (the latter title being unknown in Ireland prior to 1111) but the *Annals of Inisfallen* state that he succeeded to the Abbacy of Cork in A.D. 836. A warlike king, Feidlimid attempted to destroy the growing hegemony of the Uí Néill Kings of Leth Cuinn and waged an almost continuous war against them and their allies the Kings of Connacht and

Leinster. In A.D. 833 he attacked and destroyed the monastery of Clonmacnoise, the principal administrative centre and treasury of the Uí Briúin Kings of Connacht, sparing only the church of Saint Kieran:

> A great number of the family (religious) of Cluain-mac-noise were slain by Feidlimid, King of Cashel. and all the monastery's land was burnt by him up to the church door. In like manner did he treat the monastery of Durrow to the church door. (*Annals of the Four Masters*).

The *Annals of Ulster* preserve a contemporary verse underlining Feidlimid's military prowess:

> Feidlimid is the King
> to whom it is the work of a single day
> to un-king Connacht without a fight
> and to plunder Meath.

44:2. By A.D. 838 Feidlimid [23] was at the height of his power and forced the Uí Néill to recognise him as High-King of Ireland:

> A great assembly of the men of Ireland in Cluain Ferta Brénainn, and Niall son of Áed, King of Tara, submitted to Feidlimid, son of Crimthann, so that Feidlimid became full King of Ireland that day, and he occupied the Abbot's chair of Cluain Ferta (*Annals of Inisfallen*, sub. A.D. 838).

Within three years the Uí Néill reasserted their hegemony defeating Feidlimid at the battle of Mag Óchtair. According to an entry in the Uí Néill biased *Annals of Ulster*, unsubstantiated by the *Annals of Inisfallen* or *Annals of Clonmacnoise*, the Eóghanacht king fled the battlefield in such haste that he abandoned his crozier:

> The crozier of the devout Feidlimid, was abandoned in the blackthorns; Niall, mighty in combat, took it by right of victory in battle with swords. (*Annals of Ulster*, sub A.D. 841).

Although the crozier referred to may have appertained to Feidlimid by right of his office as Abbot of Cork, it is equally possible that it formed part of the royal regalia of Munster. The ninth-century VITA TRIPARTITA preserves a king-list of Munster which contains the curious assertion that "no one is King of Cashel until the Comarba of Patrick ordains him and gives him (holy) orders . . .and twenty-seven kings have ruled under a crozier until the time of Cenn nGécán of the seed of Ailill and Óengus." (cited by Byrne, J.F., 'Irish Kings and High-Kings,' London 1973, page 190). Although several of the Kings in question were either Bishops or Abbots the majority were not. I would posit that the expression "ruled under a crozier" may relate to the well known legend of the baptism of Óengus [3], during which Saint Patrick is said to have pierced the King's foot with his episcopal staff (see

Commentary note 24:1.). There is a distinct possibly that the crozier in question was presented by Saint Patrick to Óengus as an *éraic* or 'blood fine' in compensation for committing the crime of *eisce* or 'wounding' the king (for the brehon law on injury see: Kelly, Fergus; *A Guide to Early Irish Law*, Dublin 1988, pp. 129 - 134). Such a relic would naturally have been regarded as a powerful talisman of kingship by the Eóghanachta sovereigns and might well have been carried into battle before them in much the same manner as the *Cathach* of St. Columba served as 'the battle standard' of the O'Donnells of Tyrconnel. In this context it should be borne in mind that the VITA TRIPARTITA also states that Saint Patrick promised Óengus that none of his successors would die a violent death. Such a promise, connected with the crozier, would have strengthened its value as a spiritual validation of the temporal authority of the Eóghanacht kings.

44:4. 'Kyaran,' otherwise Saint Kieran, the Patron of Clonmacnoise. In sacking this monastery Feidlimid [23] was thought to have incurred the Saint's enmity, his death from "a great disease of the flux of the belly" in A.D. 847 being attributed to the Saint's intervention (*Annals of Clonmacnoise*). The *Annals of Inisfallen* omit any reference to St. Kieran or the cause of Feidlimid's death:

> The seventh feria (Saturday), tenth of the moon. Feidlimid, son of Crimthann, fell asleep.

Evidently Feidlimid was regarded as a Saint by the Celtic Church. The Martyrology of Donegal lists his feast day as August 28th (Op.cit., Byrne 229).

45:1. 'Ollchobhar,' or rather Ólchobar [24], was a Prince of the sept of the Eóghanacht Locha Léin. He was the great grandson of Máel Duin, King of Munster, died A.D. 786 (see Commentary note 42:1.). A cleric, like his immediate predecessor, he was Abbot of Emly. Ólchobar died in A.D. 851:

> Repose of Ólchobar son of Cináed, Abbot of Imlech Ibuir and King of Cashel (*Annals of Inisfallen*).

According to the GENEALOGIE, folio 17, Keating and MacGeoghhegan, Ólchobar fell in battle against the Norsemen, O'Dugan's 'Normans.'

46:1. 'Ailghionan,' otherwise Áilgenán [25], King of Munster, son of Donngal and grandson of Tnúthgal, King of Munster [22] (see Commentary note 43:1.) succeeded to the throne of Cashel in A.D. 851 and died in A.D. 853 (*Annals of Inisfallen*). O'Dugan is therefore wrong in ascribing to him a reign of 8 years.

46:3. 'Mhaolghuala,' or rather Máel Gualae [26], King of Munster, was the younger brother and successor of Áilgenán [25]. According to the *Annals* *of Inisfallen* he ascended the throne of Cashel in A.D. 856 which implies that there was an interregnum of some 3 years. He died in A.D. 859 after a reign of 3 years (*Annals of Inisfallen*).

47:1. 'Keann-ffaola,' or Cenn Fáelad hua Murgthigirn [27], son of Murchad, succeeded to the throne of Cashel in A.D. 859. He simultaneously held the office of Abbot of Emly. Cenn Fáelad died in A.D. 872 (*Annals of Inisfallen*).

48:2. 'Donagh,' otherwise Dúnchad [28], King of Munster. He died before A.D. 889.

49:1. 'Dubhlachta na-Tonn,' or more accurately Dub Lachtna [29], succeeded to the crown of Munster in A.D. 889 (*Annals of Inisfallen*). He was the son of Máel Gualae [26], King of Munster (see Commentary note 46:3.). His death is noted in the *Annals of Inisfallen* sub A.D. 895.

49:4. 'Ffionghuine,' otherwise Finguine Cenn nGécán [30], King of Munster son of Láegaire and nephew of King Dúnchad [28] (see Commentary note 48:2.). He was deposed in A.D. 901 in favour of Cormac macCuilennáin [31], and slain in A.D. 902 by the Cenél Conaill Chaisil (*Annals of Inisfallen*).

50:1. 'Mac Cuilionaine,' or rather Cormac mac Cuilennáin [31] succeeded to the throne of Munster in A.D. 901 (*Annals of Inisfallen*) at the deposition of Finguine Cenn nGécán [30]. He united the temporal and spiritual authorities for he was also Bishop of Emly-Cashel and therefore Metropolitan of Munster (and, from a Momonian perspective, 'Primate of all Ireland'). His last regnant ancestor was Óengus Mac Nad Froích [3] (see Commentary note 24:1), from whom he was the eleventh generation in descent, a fact underlining the elasticity of the Eóghanacht derbfhine. In A.D. 907 he forced the Southern Uí Néill and the Uí Briúin to surrender hostages thereby reasserting the theoretical balance of power between Leth Cuinn and Leth Moga. The year following, A.D. 908, he was slain at the battle of Mag Ailbe by the Uí Néill:

> The sixth feria, Friday, twenty-fourth of the moon. The battle of Mag Ailbe was gained by the Laigin and the Uí Néill over the Munstermen, in which Cormac, son of Cuilennán, King of Cashel, and Cellach son of Cerball, King of Osraige, fell. Hence a learned man said:

> Nine hundred and nine years
> From the birth of Christ - a good sign -
> Until fair Cormac fell
> In the plains of Ailbe.
> (*Annals of Inisfallen*, A.D. 909).

Geoffrey Keating (1580 - 1650) published what he believed to be the text of Cormac MacCuilennáin's Will. Although it is highly improbable to be what it purports yet we reproduce the text here as a literary curiosity:

> Summon'd away by death, which I percieve
> Approaches, (for by my prophetic skill
> I find that short will be my life and reign,)
> I solemnly appoint, that my affairs
> Shall thus be settled after I am dead;
> My golden vestment, for most sacred use
> Ordain'd, and for the service of my God,
> I give to the religious St. Shannon
> Of Inis Catha, a most holy man.
> My clock, which gave me notice of the time,
> And warn'd me when to offer my devotion,
> I leave, nor is my will to be revok'd,
> To Conuil of Feargus, a true friend,
> And follower of my fortune, good or bad.
> My Royal Robe, embroider'd o'er with gold,
> And sparkling with the rays of costly jewels,
> Well suited to a state of Majesty,
> I do bequeath to Roscrea to be kept
> by Cronane with the strictest care. My armour,
> And coat of mail of bright and polished steel,
> Will well become the martial King of Ulster,
> To whom I give it; and my Golden Chain
> Shall the most pious Machuda enjoy,
> As a reward for all his worth labours.
> My royal wardrobe I resolve to give
> To MacGleinin at Claian by Colman.
> My Psalter, which preserves the ancient records
> And monuments of this my native country,
> Which are transcrib'd with great fidelity,
> I leave to Ronan Cashel, to be preserv'd
> To after times, and ages yet to come.
> My soul for mercy I commit to heaven,
> My body leave to dust and rottenness.
> May God His choicest store of blessings send
> Upon the poor, and propagate the faith
> Of Christ throughout the world.
> (op.cit., Keating, *General History of Ireland*, page 443)

51:1. 'Fflaithbheartach,' or rather Flaithbertach mac Inmainén [32], Abbot of Inis Cathaigh succeeded Cormac mac Cuilennain on the throne of Munster. His genealogy has not been preserved but Byrne believes that he was of Múscraige rather than Eóghanacht descent (Op.cit., Byrne 204) and thus ineligible for the crown. He had acted as Cormac's chief counsellor (Op.cit., MacCarthy Mór, The., *Historical Essays on the Kingdom of Munster*, Kansas City, MO 1994, pages 45 - 46) and it is possible that he was a compromise 'care-taker' candidate chosen for the simple reason that the Eóghanachta Princes were incapable of electing an agreed candidate of their own. The GENEALOGIE, folio 27, states that Flaithbertach ascended the throne in A.D. 914 which, if true, suggests that there was an interregnum of 5 years. This would add weight to the theory that the Eóghanachta septs were too divided to elect a king from among the eligible candidates of their own dynasty. Flaithbertach's death is variously dated to A.D. 922 (*Annals of the Four Masters*) and A.D. 944 (*Annals of Inisfallen*) wherein he is not styled 'King of Cashel.' This suggests that he had either already abdicated or been deposed by his successor the Eóghanacht Chaisil Prince, Lorcán mac Coinlígaín [33].

52:1. Lorcán son of Coinlígaín was nine generations in descent from Colgu [15], King of Munster (see Commentary note 36:1.). Neither the dates of his accession or death are known.

53:1. Although it has been stated that Ceallachán Caisil [34], King of Munster, ascended the throne in A.D. 944 there is evidence to suggest that his accession occurred at least fifteen years earlier. *The Annals of Clonmacnoise* refer to him as 'King of Cashel' in an entry dated A.D. 930:

> Clonmacnoise was prayed upon by the Danes of Dublin and also it was sacrilegiously robbed afterwards by Ceallaghain, King of Cashel, and his Munstermen.

If the date given by the *Annals of Inisfallen* for the death of Flaithbertach mac Inmainán is corrupt, and he in fact died in A.D. 922 (*Annals of Ulster*), it is probable that Cellachán Caisil ascended the throne in A.D. 924. This would place the eighteen month reign of Cellachán's immediate predecessor, Lorcán, between A.D. 922 - 924.

Cellachán spent much of his reign in attempting to make a reality of Eóghanacht hegemony over Leth Moga and in crushing the pretensions of the Dál gCais (op.cit., MacCarthy Mór, *Historical Essays on the Kingdom of Munster*, pages 48 - 50). In A.D. 951 he slew Cennétig mac Lorcán, the father of Brian Bóruma. Cellachán Caisil died in A.D. 954 (*Annals of Inisfallen*) having reigned for thirty years rather than the ten ascribed to him by O'Dugan.

54:1. 'Maolfothartuighe,' otherwise Máel Fathardaig [35], King of Munster, was a tenth-generation descendant of King Fíngen [9] (see Commentary note 29:1.) who died in A.D. 619. He succeeded Cellachán Caisil in A.D. 954 but reigned for only three years. The *Annals of Inisfallen* place his death in A.D. 957.

55:1. 'Dubh-Dha-Bhoirean,' or rather Dub-Dá-Bairenn [36], King of Munster, was a Prince of the sept of the Eóghanacht Raithlind. He was no fewer

THE KINGS OF THE RACE OF EIBHEAR

than sixteen generations removed from his last royal ancestor, Conall Corc [1] (see Commentary note 21:2), a further remarkable proof of the elasticity of the Eóghanacht concept of the derbfhine. He died in A.D. 959 (*Annals of Inisfallen*) apparently at the hands of an assassin (GENEALOGIE, folio 31).

56:1. MacAilghionan,' or rather Fer Gráid [37] son of Clérech and grandson of Áilgenán [25], King of Munster (see Commentary note 46:1) succeeded to the throne in A.D. 959. Following his murder in A.D. 961 by Máolmuadh, Chief of the O'Mahonys (GENEALOGIE, folio 31), he was succeeded by his cousin Donnchad II [38], son of King Cellachán Caisil (see Commentary note 53:1).

57:1. 'Mahowne,' more usually Mathgamain [39], the first King of Munster of the usurping Dál gCais line was not the immediate successor of Fer Gráid [37]. At the latter's death he was succeeded by his cousin Donnchad II [38], son of King Cellachán Caisil [34]. Donnchad reigned for two years. He died in A.D. 963 (*Annals of Inisfallen*). Mathgamain's father, Cennétig mac Lorcán, who was slain by King Cellachán Caisil [34] in A.D. 951 (see Commentary note 53:1.) is often erroneously identified as a son of Lorcán mac Coinlígaín [33], King of Munster (see Commentary note 52:1).

57:3. The usurper Mathgamain mac Cennetig [39], 'King of Munster,' was slain in A.D. 976 by Máelmuad [40], a Prince of the sept of the Eóghanacht Raithlind (*Annals of Inisfallen*).

58:1. 'Maolmuaidh,' otherwise Máelmuad mac Brain [40] of Eóghanacht Raithlind was fourteen generations removed from his last regnant ancestor, King Feidlimid [8a] who died in 590/593. From a legitimist point of view he had every reason to be 'proud' of restoring his own dynasty to its rightful inheritance. Máelmuad was slain in A.D. 978 at the battle of Belach Lechta by Brian Bóruma, Mathgamain's brother (*Annals of Inisfallen*).

59:1. Brian Bóruma [41], brother of Mathgamain [39], usurped the throne of Munster in A.D. 978 having slain the legitimate king, Máelmuad [40], at the battle of Belach Lechta. Subsequently he claimed the High Kingship of Ireland on the spurious basis that his upstart Dál gCais dynasty were a branch of the same royal line as the Eóghanachta and thus entitled to alternate with the Uí Néill on the throne of Ireland. Brian was slain at the battle of Clontarf on Good Friday A.D. 1014. From an Eóghanacht perspective he, his predecessor, and his successors were *righ-go-freasabhra* (kings by brute force) and not *lan-righ* (legitimate kings).

60:1. 'Maolsheaclinn,' or rather Máel Sechnaill, son of Domnall. Deposed from the High Kingship by Brian Bóruma [41,] he reassumed it on the latter's death and reigned until his own in A.D. 1022.

61:3. 'Donchadh,' otherwise Donnchad [42], was a son of Brian Bóruma [41] and 'High King of Ireland, with opposition.' Deposed as 'King of Munster' and 'High King of Ireland' by his nephew, Tairrdelbach [43], he died whilst on a pilgrimage to Rome in A.D. 1064 (*Annals of Inisfallen*).

62:3. 'Toirdhealbhach,' or Tairrdelbach Ua Briain [43], son of Tadhg and grandson of Brian Bóruma [41]. He deposed his uncle, Donnchad [42], from the thrones of Munster and Ireland in A.D. 1064 and died in A.D. 1086 (*Annals of Inisfallen*). Tairrdelbach was succeeded as 'King of Munster' by his sons Tadhg [44a], who died that same year (*Annals of Inisfallen*), and Muirchertach [44], who also reigned as High-King of Ireland 'with opposition.' Muirchertach died in A.D. 1119 (*Annals of Inisfallen*) having been deposed from the High-Kingship of Ireland and the throne of Munster.

63:3. Domhnall Ua Briain [44b], grandson of Tairrdelbach [43] (see Commentary note 62:3.), was slain in A.D. 1115 by the Connachta (*Annals of Inisfallen*).

64:1. Cormac MacCarthy [46d] was the younger brother of Tadhg MacCarthy [46c], King of Desmond (died 1124), and great-great-grandson of Donnchad II [38], King of Munster at whose death, in A.D. 963, the Dál gCais usurped the throne of Munster. In A.D. 1125 Cormac besieged and destroyed Limerick, capital of the Dál gCais Kingdom of Thomond, thereby reuniting Munster under his own rule. Deposed in A.D. 1126 (*MacCarthaigh's Book*) he was restored a year later and reigned as King of Munster until his murder in 1138:

> Cormac, son of Muireadach MacCarthaigh, King of the two provinces of Munster (i.e. Desmond and Thomond), and defender of all Leth Moga, the most pious and valorous of men, the best for bestowing food and clothes, was, after building the church of Cormac at Cashel and twelve churches at Lismore, treacherously killed by Diarmaid Súgach son of Mathghamhain Ó Conchobhair Ciarraighe and Ó Talcin, at the instigation of Toirdhealbhach son of Diarmaid Ó Briain, in his own house at Magh Tamnach (op.cit., hInnse, *MacCarthaigh's Book*, sub: 1138).

> The most successful Eóghanacht King in several centuries Cormac, at the height of his power, was able to enforce the abdication of Toirdhealbhach Ó Conchobhar, King of Connacht, as High-King of Ireland in A.D. 1134 (Op.cit., MacCarthy Mór, *Historical Essays on the Kingdom of Munster*, pages 53 - 54).

64:2. Domhnall Ua Briain [44b], 'King of Munster,' died in A.D. 1115. He was the son of Tadhg Ua Briain [44a], 'King of Munster,' who died in A.D. 1086.

66:1. This verse has obviously been displaced. It refers to Tairrdelbach Ua Briain [43], High-King of Ireland and 'King of Munster' who died in A.D. 1086 (see Commentary note 62:3.).

67:1. Another displaced verse. Muircheartach Ua Briain [44] was 'King of Munster' and High-King of Ireland (see Commentary note 62:3.). He died in A.D. 1119.

68:2. 'Diermott O'Brien,' otherwise Diarmait Ua Briain [45], younger brother and immediate successor of Muircheartach Ua Briain [44] (deposed 1118). He died in A.D. 1118, a few months after his succession as King of Thomond (*Annals of Inisfallen*).

69:1. 'Connor O'Brien,' or rather Conchobhar-na-Catharach Ua Brian, son of Diarmait Ua Briain [45] (see Commentary note 68:2.) succeeded his father as King of Thomond. In 1127 he, and his brother, Tairrdealbach [46], acknowledged Cormac MacCarthy [46d] as King of Munster:

> Conchobhar and Tairrdealbach, two sons of Diarmait Ua Briain, turned against Toirdhealbhach son of Raidhri (Ó Conchobhair, otherwise O'Connor) and went to Lismore, and clasped hands with Cormac MacCarthaigh (i.e. they swore an oath of fealty), and brought him back to life again (i.e. out of the monastery). He took the kingship of Munster again, and banished Donnchadh son of Mac Carthaigh to Connacht. (op.cit., Ó hInnse, 'MacCarthaigh's Book').

> Ó Conchobhar died in A.D. 1142 (MacCarthaigh's Book).

70:1. A displaced verse. Tadhg MacCarthy [46c] was the elder brother of Cormac MacCarthy [46d] (died 1138) who restored Eóghanacht rule in Desmond, or South Munster, in 1118. Toirdhealbhach O'Brien, otherwise Tairrdelbach Ua Briain [46], is not to be confused with the king of the same name who died in A.D. 1086. He was the latter's grandson, his father being Diarmait Ua Briain [45], King of Thomond, who died in A.D. 1118. Tadhg MacCarthy abdicated the crown of Desmond to his younger brother, Cormac, in A.D. 1123 and died of an incurable disease that same year:

> Ó Mathghamhna, Ó Súilleabhain, Ó Caoimh, Ó Muircheartaigh and Ó Fáolain deposed Tadhg, son of Muireadach MacCarthaigh; and Cormac son of Mac Carthaigh, his own brother, took the kingship from them in his presence... Tadhg, son of Muireadhach son of Carthach son of Saoirbhreathach, died penitently at Cashel. (op. cit., Ó hInnse, MacCarthaigh's Book, sub: 1123)

71:1. The 'Mortagh' in question would appear to have been Muichertach Ua Briain [47], 'King of Munster' and Thomond (obit. 1168), son of Tairrdelbach Ua Briain [46], 'King of Munster' and Thomond (obit. 1167).

71:4. 'Donell,' or rather Domnall Mór Ua Briain [47a], King of Thomond (obit. 1194), son of Tairrdelbach Ua Briain [46] (obit. 1167), and brother of Muirchertach Ua Briain (obit. 1168).

80:2. 'Mac Alpruinn,' literally 'son of Alpruinn,' a corruption of 'Calpurnius.' In his 'Confession' Saint Patrick stated that he was the son of "Calpurnius, a deacon, son of Potitus, a priest, of the village of Bannavem Taburniae..."

80:3. Cashel is here presented as the 'vicarage' of Saint Patrick, which is to say as his primatial See.

80:4. Cashel had been specifically identified with Patrick since the fifth century. The Bishop-Abbots of Emly-Cashel were regarded, in a particular sense, not only as the *comarba* or 'successors' of Saint Ailbe but also of Saint Patrick. Accordingly they saw themselves as both Metropolitans of Munster and Primates of Leth Mogha if not of all Ireland. This spiritual claim was the counterpart of the temporal claims of the Eóghanacht kings, and indeed they reinforced each other. This is made explicit in the late eleventh-century manuscript known as *Lebor na gCeart*, which bluntly asserts that Cashel was blessed by God, through the Angel Victor, as the See of Patrick and Seat of the High Kings of Ireland:

> In the time of Corc son of Lugaid two swineheards happened to frequent that hill (of Cashel) for a period of three months, masting their swine... and they beheld a form bright as the sun with a voice sweet as a lute, blessing the hill and the place... That form was Patrick's angel Victor, prophesying Patrick, and proclaiming that the dignity and primacy of Ireland would always be in that place. Accordingly it is Patrick's Sanctuary and the principal stronghold of the King of Ireland. And the rent and service of the men of Ireland is due to the King of that place always, namely to the King of Cashel through the blessing of Patrick son of Calpurnius. (Dillon. Myles, ed: 'Lebor na gCert, The Book of Rights,' Irish Texts Society, 1984, pages 4 - 5).

The See of Emly-Cashel ignored the spiritual pretensions of Uí Néill Armagh, just as the Eóghanacht Kings ignored the temporal claims of their Uí Néill rivals to the High-Kingship. Eóghanacht Munster was deeply committed to the ideal of its own complete temporal and spiritual sovereignty (see Commentary note 43:1.)

81:1. 'Diarmuid MacCarthy,' or, more properly, Diarmait MacCarthaigh [47b], King of Desmond (reg. 1144 - 1185) was the eldest son of Cormac MacCarthy [46d], King of Munster (obit. 1138). As head of the Eóghanachta he claimed the title 'King of Munster' although in reality his authority was confined to South Munster, or Desmond. In a Royal Charter granted circa 1173 to the Monastery of St. John the Evangelist,

Cork, Diarmait was styled "by favour of Divine Clemency, King of Munster." (op. cit. MacCarthy Mór, *Historical Essays on the Kingdom of Munster*, pages 199-121). By implication O'Dugan regarded the Eóghanacht Diarmait MacCarthy and his descendants as the "rightful King(s) of Cashel," which is to say of Munster.

The Kings of the Race of Eibhear

APPENDIX ONE
A SUCCESSIONAL LIST OF THE KINGS OF MUNSTER

The following 'King List' is based on the succession roll of the Kings of Munster published by Professor F.J. Byrne in his seminal work *Irish Kings and High Kings*. Joint and overlapping reigns, as well as those of 'Kings with Opposition,' have been treated as a single subdivided reign. In each case the verse and line numbers in which a particular sovereign is referred to by O'Dugan is cited. It is a remarkable fact that, prior to the Dál gCais usurpation, O'Dugan displays an ignorance of only the most obscure of the Eóghanacht Kings almost all of whom were merely 'associated on the throne' with a more important figure, or who reigned briefly as minor 'kings with opposition.' In many cases, such as those of Feidlimid (8a), Tuathal (21a) and Tnúthgal (22) even Professor Byrne has been unable to adduce any reliable historical data on these kings save only their probable genealogical affiliations.

Following the Dál gCais usurpation O'Dugan's 'King List' becomes less reliable. Several Ua Briain kings are simply omitted. This may reflect a pro-Eóghanacht bias on the part of the poet, a supposition made more probable by the fact that in the last quatrain he concludes by praising Diarmait MacCarthaigh, and by implication his successors, as the "rightful King(s) of Cashel."

SEMI-HISTORICAL KINGS OF MUNSTER WHO REIGNED PRIOR TO THE FOUNDATION OF CASHEL

Mug Nuadat, alias Eóghan Taidlech, alias Eóghan Fitheccach	1:1; 11:1; 12:1
Ailill Ólomm	2:1; 14:1
Eóghan Mór	2:2
Cian	3:1
Cormac Cass	3:1; 15:1
Fiachu Mullethan	3:3; 16:1
Mogha Corb	17:1
Ailill Fland Bec	4:1; 19:1
Luightech	4:3

The Kings of the Race of Eibhear

HISTORICAL KINGS OF MUNSTER
FROM THE FOUNDATION OF CASHEL
UNTIL THE ADVENT OF THE ANGLO NORMANS

1.	Conall Corc	5:1; 21:2
2.	Nad Froích mac Cuirc	22:1
3.	Óengus mac Nad Froích (Obit. 490/492)	23:1; 24:1
3a.	Dauí Iarlaithe mac Maithni	
4.	Eochaid mac Óengusso	24:1
4a.	Dub Gilcach mac Óengusso	
4b.	Feidlimid I mac Óengusso	
5.	Crimthann Srem mac Echdach	25:1
6.	Coirpre Cromm	26:2; 28:1; 31:3
7.	Fergus Scandal	27:1
8.	Feidlimid II mac Coirpri	28:1
8a.	Feidlimid III mac Tigernaig (Obit. 590/593)	
8b.	Amalgaid mac Éndai	30:4
8c.	Garbán mac Éndai	30:2
9.	Fíngen I mac Áedo Duib (Obit. 619)	29:1
9a.	Áed Bennán mac Crimthainn (Obit. 619/621)	31:2
10.	Cathal I mac Áedo (Obit. 628)	32:1
11.	Faílbe Fland (Obit. 637/639)	33:1
12.	Cúan mac Amalgado (Obit. 641)	34:1
13.	Máenach mac Fíngin (Obit. 662)	34:3
14.	Cathal II Cú-cen-máthair (Obit. 641)	35:1
15.	Colgú mac Faílbi Fland (Obit. 678)	36:1
16.	Fínguine II mac Cathail Cú-cen-máthair (Obit. 695/696)	37:1
16a.	Ailill mac Cathail (Obit. 698/701)	
17.	Eterscél mac Máele Umai (Obit. 721)	38:1; 41:4
18.	Cormac I mac Ailello (Obit. 713)	39:1
19.	Cathal III mac Fínguine (Obit. 742)	40:1
20.	Cathussach mac Eterscélai	41:1
20a.	Máel Duin mac Áedo (Obit. 786)	42:1
20b.	Ólchobar I mac Flainn (Obit. 796/7)	
20c.	Ólchobar II mac Duib-Indrecht (Obit. 805)	
21.	Artrí mac Cathail (Obit. 821	43:1
21a.	Tuathal mac Artoig	
22.	Tnúthgal mac Donngaile	
23.	Feidlimid IV mac Crimthainn (Obit. 847)	44:1
24.	Ólchobar III mac Cinaeda (Obit. 851)	45:1
25.	Áilgenán mac Donngaile (Obit. 853)	46:1
26.	Máel Gualae mac Donngaile (Obit. 859)	46:3
27.	Cenn Fáelad hua Mugthigirn (Obit. 872)	47:1
28.	Dúnchad I mac Duib-dá-Bairenn (Obit. 888)	48:2
29.	Dub Lachtna mac Máele Gualae (Obit. 895)	49:1

The Kings of the Race of Eibhear

30. Finguine III Cenn nGécán mac Lóegairi (Obit. 902)   49:4
31. Cormac II mac Cuilennáin (Obit. 908)   50:1
32. Flaithbertach mac Inmainén (Obit. 944)   51:1
33. Lorcán mac Coinlígaín   52:1
34. Cellachán Caisil mac Buadacháin (Obit. 954)   53:1
35. Máel Fathardaig mac Flainn (Obit. 957)   54:1
36. Dub-dá-Baireen mac Domnaill (Obit. 959)   55:1
37. Fer Gráid mac Clérig (Obit. 961)   56:1
38. Donnchad II mac Cellacháin (Obit. 963)
39. Mathgamain mac Cennétig (Obit. 976)   57:1
40. Máelmuad mac Brain (Obit. 978)   58.1
41. Brian Bóruma mac Cennétig (Obit. 1014)   59:1
41a. Dúngal mac Máelfothartaig Hua Donnchada (Obit. 1025)
42. Donnchad mac Briain (Obit. 1064)   61:3
42a. Murchad mac Donnchada (Obit. 1068)
43. Tairrdelbach hua Briain (Obit. 1086)   62:3
44. Muirchertach Ua Briain (Obit. 1119)   71:1
44a. Tadhg mac Tairrdelbaig Ua Briain (Obit. 1086)
44b. Domnall mac Taidg Ua Briain (Obit. 1115)   63:3
45. Diarmait mac Tairrdelbaig Ua Briain (Obit. 1118)
46. Tairrdelbach mac Diarmata Ua Briain (Obit. 1167)   70:2
46a. Brian mac Murchada Ua Briain (Obit. 1118)
46b. Tadhg Gláe Ua Briain (Obit. 1118)
46c. Tadhg MacCarthaigh (Obit. 1124)   70:1
46d. Cormac MacCarthaigh (Obit. 1138)   64:1
47. Muirchertach Ua Briain (Obit. 1168)
47a. Domnall Mór Ua Briain (Obit 1194)   71:3; 74:2
47b. Diarmaid MacCarthaigh (Obit. 1185)   81:1

The Kings of the Race of Eibhear

APPENDIX TWO
GENEALOGICAL CHARTS OF THE EÓGHANACHT AND DÁL gCAIS KINGS OF MUNSTER

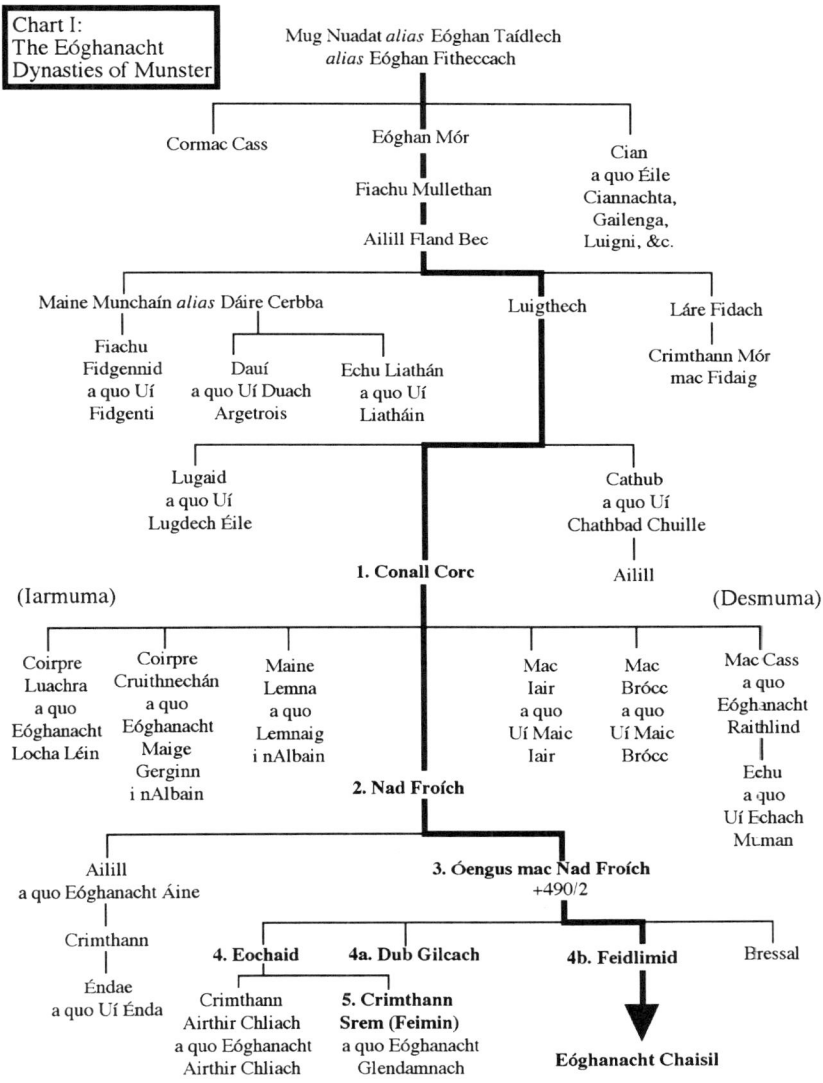

Chart I: The Eóghanacht Dynasties of Munster

The Kings of the Race of Eibhear

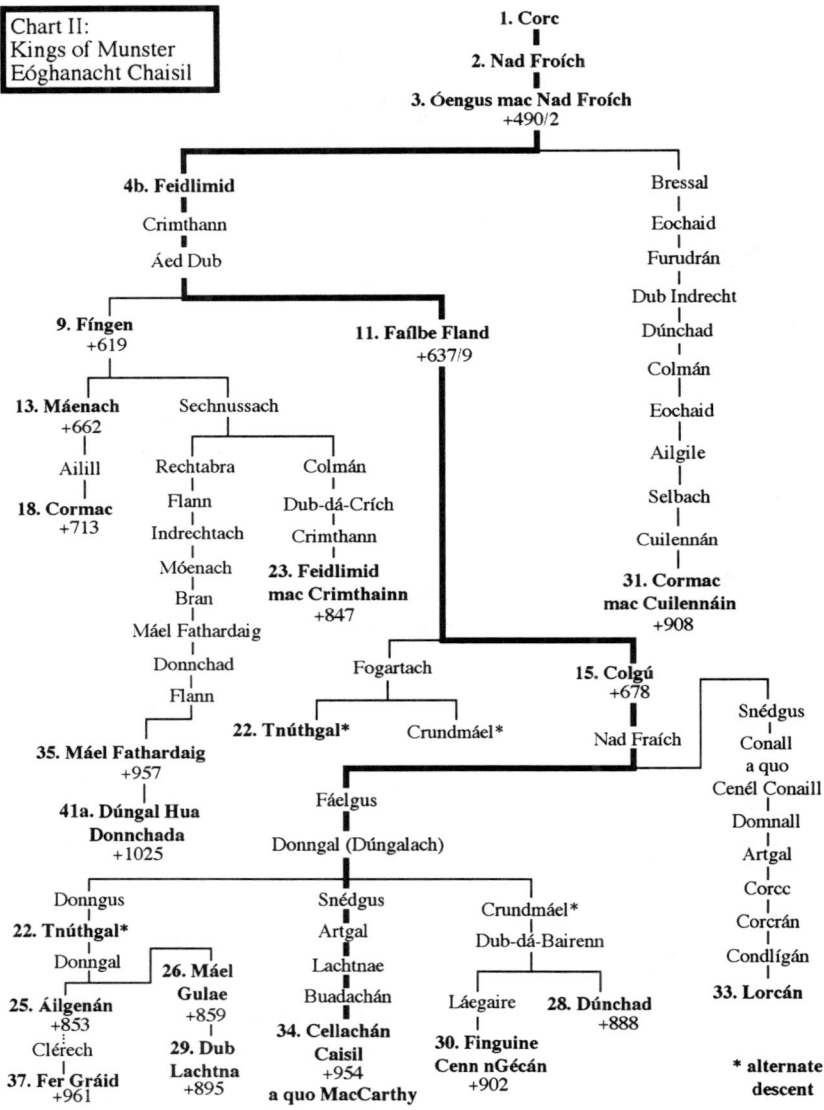

Chart II: Kings of Munster Eóghanacht Chaisil

The Kings of the Race of Eibhear

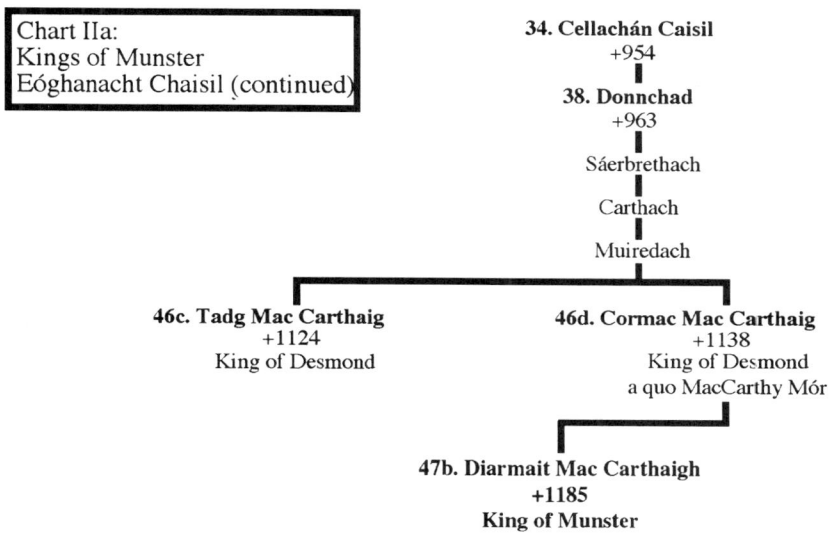

Chart IIa:
Kings of Munster
Eóghanacht Chaisil (continued)

34. **Cellachán Caisil**
+954

38. **Donnchad**
+963

Sáerbrethach

Carthach

Muiredach

46c. **Tadg Mac Carthaig**
+1124
King of Desmond

46d. **Cormac Mac Carthaig**
+1138
King of Desmond
a quo MacCarthy Mór

47b. **Diarmait Mac Carthaigh**
+1185
King of Munster

The Kings of the Race of Eibhear

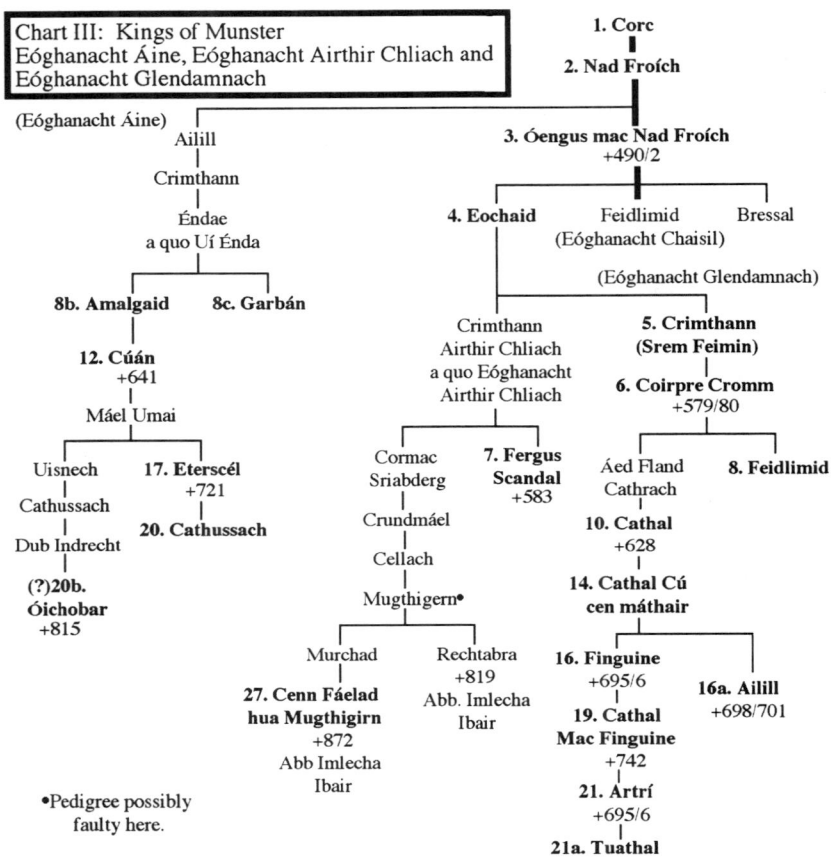

Chart III: Kings of Munster
Eóghanacht Áine, Eóghanacht Airthir Chliach and
Eóghanacht Glendamnach

THE KINGS OF THE RACE OF EIBHEAR

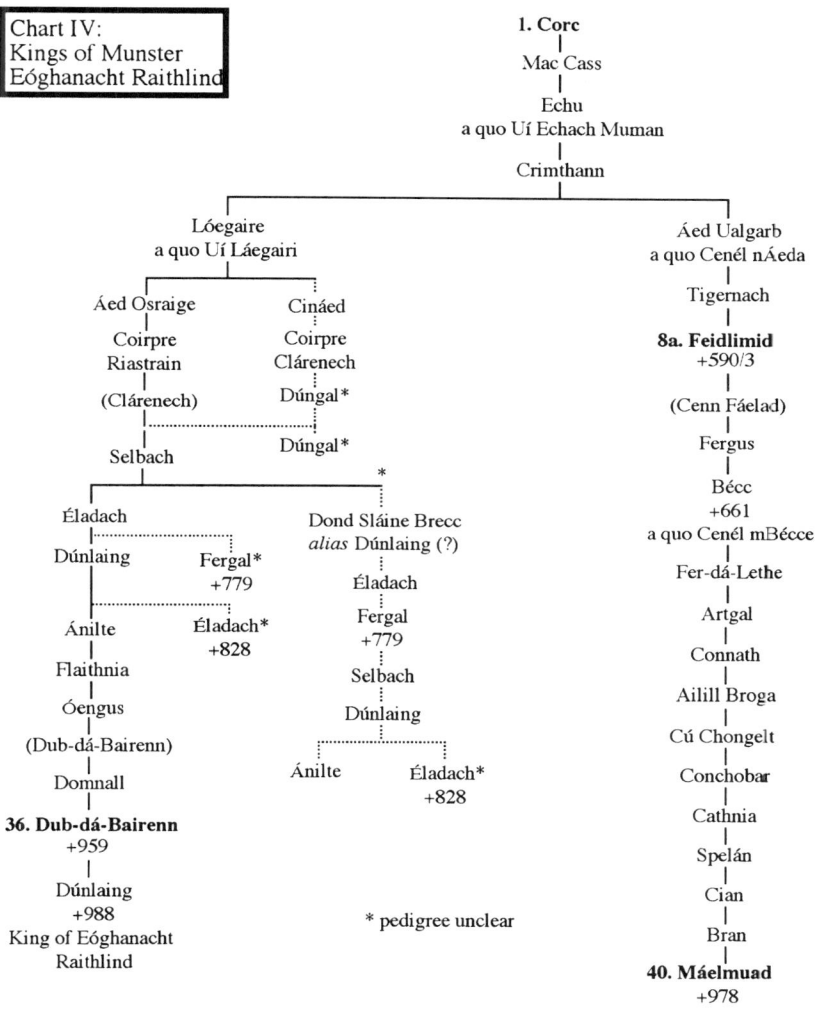

Chart IV:
Kings of Munster
Eóghanacht Raithlind

The Kings of the Race of Eibhear

Chart V:
Kings of Munster
Eóghanacht Locha Léin

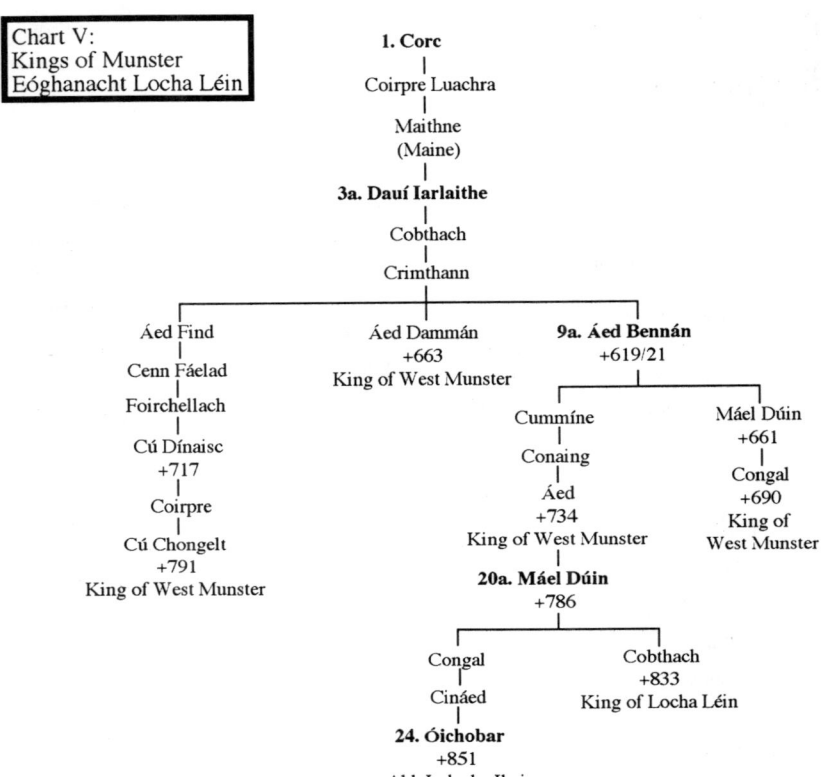

THE KINGS OF THE RACE OF EIBHEAR

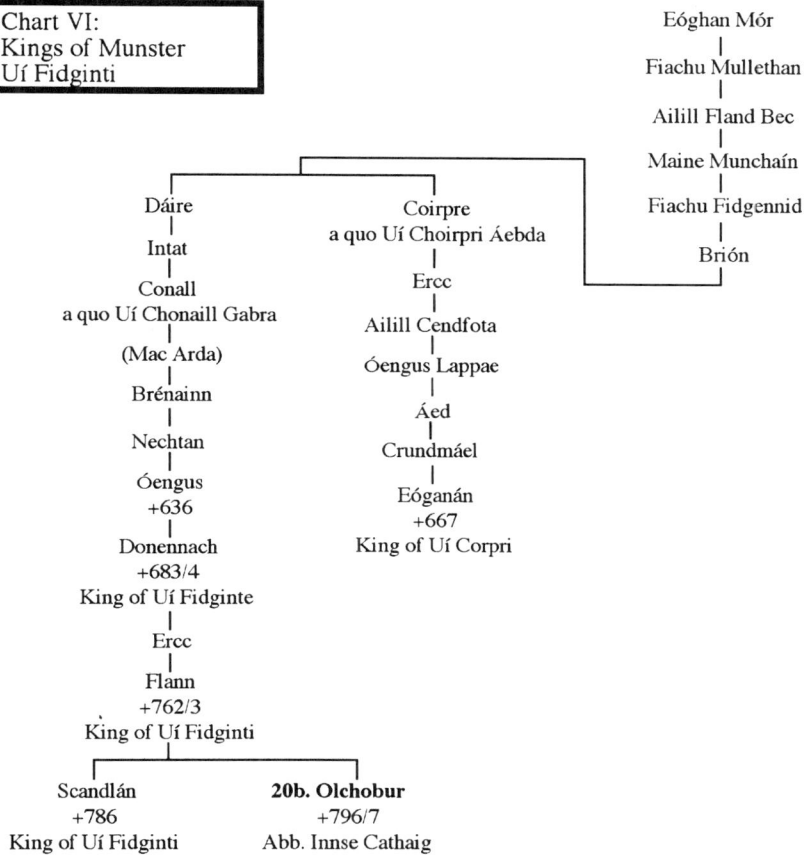

Chart VI:
Kings of Munster
Uí Fidginti

The Kings of the Race of Eibhear

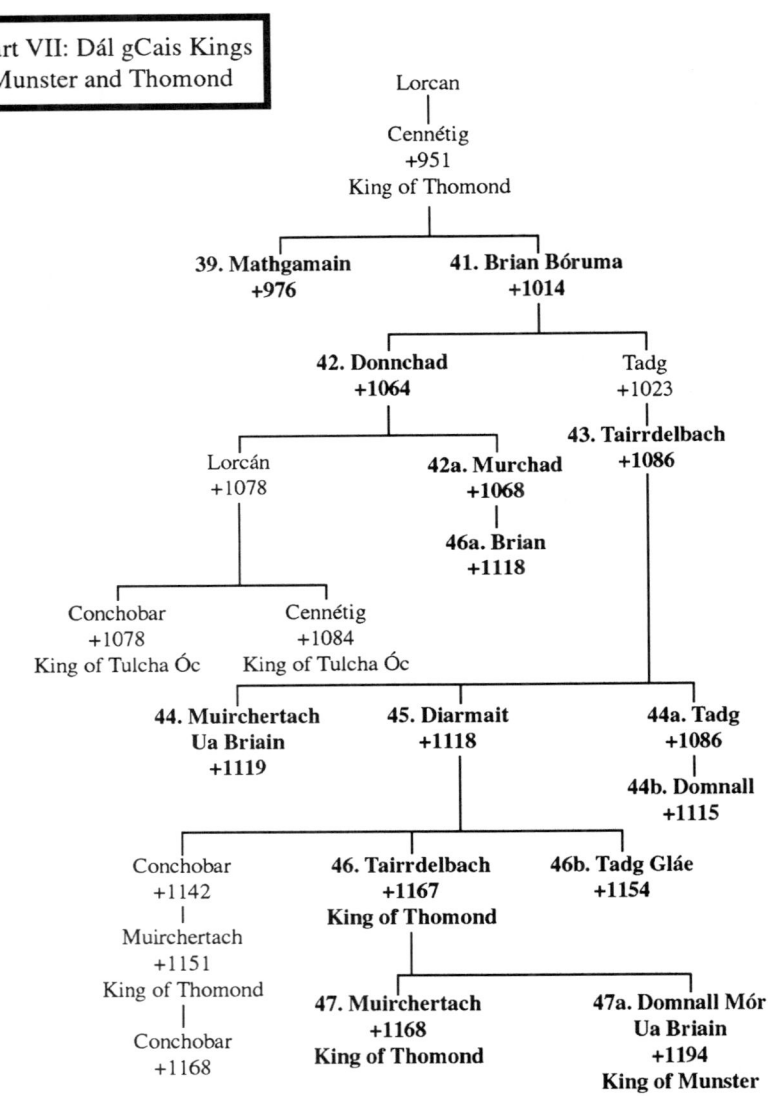

Chart VII: Dál gCais Kings of Munster and Thomond

APPENDIX THREE
THE DESCENT OF CONALL CORC FROM
EIBHEAR AND MILESIUS

Although O'Dugan's poem is entitled 'THE KINGS OF THE RACE OF EIBHEAR' it is remarkable for the fact that he neither relates the history of that supposed ancestor of the Eóghanachta nor details their descent from him. Had the poet entitled his work 'THE KINGS OF THE RACE OF EÓGHAN MÓR' these omissions would not concern us in as much as this is the subject matter of the poem; but it is problematic that the poem, as now constituted, makes no reference to the Milesian ancestry of the Momonian kings, and specifically to their Eibhearian descent. One possible explanation for these omissions is that the poem is not in fact complete and that earlier stanzas have been lost. This may be supported by the fact that the opening quatrain specifically concerns Cashel, and that the poem as a whole is a king-list of those sovereigns who reigned from the Rock. It would have been entirely natural for the translator, Michael Kearney, the scion of a Gaelic noble family based in Cashel, to have concentrated on that portion of the poem dealing with the foundation of the city as the seat of the Eóghanacht kings whilst omitting stanzas dealing with the Eibhearian ancestry of those sovereigns, a descent well known to his contemporaries.

The Eóghanachta, in common with the other Gaelic Royal Houses, are of Milesian descent which is to say that they claimed male line descent from Milesius or 'Mile Easpain' ('A Soldier of Spain'), the semi-mythical progenitor of the Gaelic nobility. Much ink has been expended on whether Míle Easpain was or was not an historical character. This debate is irrelevant. The important point, preserved in his 'name,' is that it establishes that the Gaelic Irish preserved a 'race memory' that their earliest ancestors had migrated into Ireland from Spain, a fact confirmed by archaeology (Berresford Ellis, Peter, *The Ancient World of the Celts*, London 1998, page 223). This 'race memory' was undoubtedly preserved in an oral form for centuries before it was committed to writing in *Leabhar Gabhála* or 'The Book of Invasions.' We need not discuss here the supposed history of Milesius and his descendants. This is easily accessible in any number of works including Geoffrey Keating's *General History of Ireland*. However, to complement O'Dugan's poem, the king-list printed in Appendix One, and the genealogical tables given in Appendix Two, I reproduce below the traditional descent of Conall Corc, first King of Cashel, from Milesius and Eibhear.

Milesius, 'King of Galicia,' father of
Eibhear (normally anglicised as Heber) his eldest surviving son, King of Leth

The Kings of the Race of Eibhear

    Moga, father of
Conmaol, King of Ireland for 30 years, father of
Eochaidh Faobharglas, King of Ireland for 20 years, father of
Rosa, father of
Nuagatt Deaghlamh, father of
Glas, father of
Rotheachta, King of Ireland for 25 years,
Irereorda, father of
Casclothach, King of Munster for 13 years, father of
Muinheamhoin, King of Ireland for 5 years, founder of The Niadh Nasc,
    father of
Aildergoid, King of Ireland for 7 years, father of
Cas Cead Chaigneach, King of Munster for 36 years, father of
Failbhe, King of Munster for 26 years, father of
Roane, father of
Rotheachta, King of Ireland for 7 years, father of
Elim, King of Ireland for 1 year, father of
Art Imleach, King of Ireland for 22 years, father of
Breasrigh, King of Ireland for 9 years, father of
Seadhna Jonaraice, King of Ireland for 20 years, father of
Duach Fionn, King of Ireland for 5 years, father of
Eadhna Dearg, King of Ireland for 12 years, father of
Luighaidh Jarhoinn, King of Ireland for 9 years, father of
Eochaidh Vairceas, King of Ireland for 12 years, father of
Luighaidh Lamhdhearg, King of Ireland for 7 years, father of
Art, King of Ireland for 6 years, father of
Oilioll Fionn, King of Ireland for 9 years, father of
Eochaidh, King of Ireland for 7 years, father of
Lughaidh Laighe, King of Ireland for 7 years, father of
Reachta Righdhearg, King of Ireland for 20 years, father of
Cobhthaigh Caomh, King of Munster for 29 years, father of
Modchorb, King of Ireland for 7 years, father of
Fearchorb, King of Ireland for 11 years, father of
Adamhar, King of Ireland for 5 years, father of
Niadh Seadhamhuin, King of Ireland for 7 years, father of
Jonadhmhar, King of Ireland for 3 years, father of
Luighaidh Laighne, King of Ireland for 5 years, father of
Cairbre Cuisgleathan, King of Munster for 28 years, father of
Duach Donn Dalta Deagha, King of Ireland for 10 years, father of
Eochaidh Garb, King of Munster for 30 years, father of
Muireach, King of Munster for 17 years, father of
Modhafeibhis, father of
Luigheach Móre, King of Munster for 2 years, father of
Eana Munchaoin, King of Munster for 10 years, father of
Deirgthine, King of Munster for 13 years, father of

Deary, father of
Modha Neid, King of Munster for 23 years, father of
Eóghan Mór, King of Munster for 15 years, father of
Ailill Olomm, King of Munster for 27 years, father of
Eóghan Mór, King of Munster, father of
Faichu Mullethan, King of Munster, father of
Ailill Fland Bec, King of Munster, father of
Luighthech, King of Munster, father of
Conall Corc, King of Munster, founder of Cashel.

The Kings of the Race of Eibhear

APPENDIX FOUR
NOTES ON JOHN DALY'S PREFACE TO THE 1847 EDITION

In his preface to the 1847 edition of 'THE KINGS OF THE RACE OF EIBHEAR' Mr. Daly erroneously dates the composition of O'Dugan's poem to 1367 on the basis of a supposed reference to Toirdhealbhach O'Brien, King of Thomond (reg. 1369 - 1375) in line two of the seventieth quatrain: 'Toirdealbhach O'Brien, a sovereign prince.' There can be little doubt that this identification is entirely wrong. In the year in question Mathghamhain O'Brien was King of Thomond (reg. 1360-69) and whilst he was eventually succeeded by his younger brother Toirdhealbhach Maol (reg. 1369 - 1375, died 1398) the latter cannot be the object of O'Dugan's remarks. It is evident from the fact that the poet juxtaposes the reigns of Tadhg MacCarthy (reg. 1118 - 1123) and 'Toirdhealbach O'Brien, a sovereign prince' that he was in fact referring to Tairrdelbach Ua Briain who ascended the throne of Thomond in 1118, and thus was exactly contemporaneous with the Eóghanacht Sovereign. All that can be said for certain on the dating of O'Dugan's poem is that it cannot be later than 1372, the year in which he died according to the *Annals of the Four Masters*.

O'Dugan's poem, as reproduced in this book, was translated from the Gaelic by "Michael Kearney, of Ballyloskye, in the County of Crosse Tipperary". Daly offers little information concerning the translator but it is immediately evident, from the fact that he could both read and write in Gaelic and English, that he had received a formal education and thus came of 'good family.' The townland of 'Ballyloskye' corresponds with that of Ballylusky, in the parish of Magowry, and Barony of Middlethird, County Tipperary. It formed part of the estates of the O'Kearneys of Cashel, a well known family of Gaelic nobility long settled in the capital of the Eóghanacht Kings.

It is obvious, from the conclusion to the last quatrain, that Kearney completed his translation of O'Dugan's poem in Cashel. This underlines his almost certain connection with the O'Kearneys of that city. Given this fact, and the evidence of his education, I would posit that our translator may have been none other than Michael O'Kearney (born 1588) a younger son of Patrick O'Kearney, Chief of his Name and Arms, who died on April 22nd 1641 (MacCarthy Mór, The., *Ulster's Office 1552-1800*, Gryfons 1996, page 197), and thus the direct ancestor of the von O'Kearneys of Austria and the Comtes de Kearnies of France (von Dassanowsky, Professor Robert., 'The O'Kearney of Cashel: From Beginnings to the Austrian Empire,' in *The Augustan*, Volume XXV, Number 4, Issue 108, pages 10-15). Needless to say the O'Kearneys of Cashel were of Milesian and Eibhearian descent numbering both Mug Nuadat (Commentary note 1:1) and Ailill Ólomm (Commentary note 2:1) among their male line ancestors, facts which may well have encouraged Michael Kearney to undertake this translation.

LINKS IN A GOLDEN CHAIN
Collected Essays on the History of The Niadh Nask or the Order of the Golden Chain
edited by The Count of Clandermond
With a foreword by Peter Berresford Ellis for the Royal Eóghanacht Society

- A History of The Niadh Nask, or the Military Order of the Golden Chain by The MacCarthy Mór, Prince of Desmond
- The Celtic Warrior Tradition by Peter Berresford Ellis
- Niadh Nask References in Two Twelfth Century Manuscripts, Caithreim Cheallachain Chaisil & The Vision of Tnugdal by The MacCarthy Mór, Prince of Desmond
- The Bardic Class and the Gaelic Concept of Nobility by Office by Dr. Patrick O'Shea of Tiraha
- The Niadh Nask Bookplates of a Duke, A Marquis and an Hereditary Saint by The Count of Clandermond
- A Binding with Chains, The Rite of Investiture of The Niadh Nask by The MacCarthy Mór, Prince of Desmond
- Lament for a Kingdom, The Poetry of Egan O'Rahilly by The Count of Clandermond
- Chains and Crosses, The Insignia of The Niadh Nask by An Tanaiste Eóghan MacCarthy
- Speculations on the Shrine of Lemanaghan: Battle Banner of The Niadh Nask? by The MacCarthy Mór, Prince of Desmond and Dr. Patrick O'Shea of Tiraha
- A Niadh Nask "In Memoria Roll" of Five Reigns by An Rioghdamna Conor M. MacCarthy
- Knights of a Different Hue, The Anglo-Norman Hereditary Knights of the Palatinate Earldom of Desmond by The MacCarthy Mór, Prince of Desmond
- The Arms of The Niadh Nask by The McKerrell of Hillhouse
- Some Early American Niadh Nask by An Rioghdamna Conor MacCarthy
- Divisions of Colour by An Tanaiste Eóghan MacCarthy
- The Recognition of The Niadh Nask by the International Commission for Orders of Chivalry by Lieutenant Colonel Baron O'Kelly de Conejera
- The Establishment of The Niadh Nask in North America by Dr. David Pittman Johnson of Kilbonane

Appendices
- Preface to The Niadh Nask History & International Roll 1996 by Lord Borthwick
- Extract: International Commission for Orders of Chivalry 1996 Edition
- Descent of The MacCarthy Mór, Prince of Desmond from Muinheamhoin
- The Niadh Nask and The International Commission for Orders of Chivalry, A Supplementary Note to the 1978 ICOC Register by Lieutenant Colonel Baron O'Kelly de Conejera
- The Niadh Nask and The Standing Council of Irish Chiefs and Chieftains by The Count of Clandermond
- An Early American Literary Reference to The Niadh Nask by The Count of Clandermond

210+ pages, illustrated; index ISBN 096542202X
LIMITED EDITION OF 200 HARDBOUND COPIES
US$40 postpaid (US$50 non-US Customers postpaid airmail)

LIMITED EDITION OF 300 CARD COVER COPIES
US$30 postpaid (US$40 non-US Customer postpaid airmail)

THE MACCARTHYS OF MUNSTER
The History of a Great Irish Sept
by Samuel Trant MacCarthy Mór, D.L., J.P., M.R.I.A. (first published 1922)

With an extended commentary thereon by The MacCarthy Mór, Prince of Desmond

Gryfons is proud to announce the release of a facsimile edition of this rare and much sought after historical and genealogical account of the Royal House of MacCarthy Mór and its many cadet lines. Widely greeted in 1922 as the most extensive history of Clan MacCarthy attempted to that date, this second edition is complemented by the addition of an extensive commentary, correcting errors in the original work, updating pedigrees and incorporating previously unpublished archival material from the family papers.

570+ pages, illustrated with plates of family portraits, castles, and seats, indexed; bibliography; ISBN 0965422011
US$60 postpaid (US$70 non-US Customers postpaid airmail)

A NEW BOOK OF RIGHTS
(LEABHAR NA GCEART NUA)

Being a Complete Transcript of the Legal Verdicts Handed Down by the Courts of the Republic of Italy Concerning the Heraldic Rights, Status and Prerogatives of The MacCarthy Mór, Prince of Desmond, Chief of his Name and Arms and Head of the Eóghanacht Royal House of Munster

With a Translation of Letters Patent confirming the same issued by His Excellency The Marques de la Floresta, Castile & Leon King of Arms

With an historical introduction by Peter Berresford Ellis and Legal Commentaries by The Hon. Chief Judge J. M. Johnson, NN, BA, MA, SJD; H.E. Capt. The Chev. M. L. Lathrop of Castlecormac, USNR, Ret., JD; and The Hon. D. V. Brooks of Ardea, NN, BA, JD

@ 150+ pages • illustrated card cover • ISBN 0965422046
LIMITED EDITION OF 250 PAPERBACK COPIES
US$30 postpaid (US$40 non-US Customers postpaid airmail)

AN IRISH MISCELLANY
Essays Heraldic, Historical and Genealogical
by The MacCarthy Mór, Prince of Desmond and The Count of Clandermond

Contents
- The Greening of Irish History, *The MacCarthy Mór, Prince of Desmond*
- Saint Patrick's Crown, *The MacCarthy Mór, Prince of Desmond*
- Monarchy, The Forgotten Sacrament, *The MacCarthy Mór, Prince of Desmond*
- The High Kingship of Ireland; An Examination of Historical Evidences, *The MacCarthy Mór, Prince of Desmond*
- Gaelic Heraldry and the Kingdom of Desmond, *The Count of Clandermond*
- Gaelic Heraldry and the Kingdom of Desmond: Some Further Notes, *The Count of Clandermond*
- The Chief Herald of Ireland and the Nobiliary Status of Irish Arms, *The MacCarthy Mór, Prince of Desmond*
- Shields, Ensigns and Standards; Proto-Heraldry in Gaelic Ireland, *The MacCarthy Mór, Prince of Desmond*
- Hatchments and Heralds: A Brief Account of Funeral Practices in Ireland, *The MacCarthy Mór, Prince of Desmond*
- Gaelic Feudalism and the Kingdom of Desmond, *The Count of Clandermond*
- The Liberal Policy of Lord Deputy St. Leger and the Foundation of Ulster's Office, *The MacCarthy Mór, Prince of Desmond*
- King Donal IX MacCarthy Mór, A Political Portrait, *The Count of Clandermond*
- "She Engaged Him to Surrender into Her Hands His Kingdom of Desmond" King Donal IX MacCarthy Mór and Elizabeth Tudor, *The Count of Clandermond*
- A Brief Genealogical Account of The Maguires, Princes of Fermanagh and Barons of Enniskillen, *The MacCarthy Mór, Prince of Desmond*
- A Brief Pedigree of the Chiefly House of the O'Doghertys of Inishowen, *The MacCarthy Mór, Prince of Desmond*
- A Brief Account of the Eóghanacht Chiefs and Their Clans, *The Count of Clandermond*
- The O'Longs of Garranelongy, *The MacCarthy Mór, Prince of Desmond*
- The Fergusons of Belfast: A Short Account of the Ancestry of H.R.H. The Duchess of York, *The MacCarthy Mór, Prince of Desmond*
- "By the Help of Many Lies," or How Penal Were the Penal Laws?, *The MacCarthy Mór, Prince of Desmond*
- Irish Heraldic Bookplates, *The Count of Clandermond*
- The Order of St. Patrick — Why It Cannot Be "Restored" by the Irish Republic, *The MacCarthy Mór, Prince of Desmond*
- The Genealogical Importance of the Public Record Office of Northern Ireland, *The MacCarthy Mór, Prince of Desmond and The Count of Clandermond*
- The "Auctoritas" and "Potestas" of Princes; Divine Gift or Popular Concession?", *The MacCarthy Mór, Prince of Desmond*

350 pages • illustrated library cover • Indexed with bibliography • ISBN 0965422038

LIMITED EDITION OF 200 HARDBOUND COPIES
US$40 postpaid (US$50 non-US Customers postpaid airmail)

LIMITED EDITION OF 300 CARD COVER COPIES
US$30 postpaid (US$40 non-US Customer postpaid airmail)

THREE CENTURIES OF NIADH NASK BOOKPLATES
by The Count of Clandermond
With a foreword by The MacCarthy Mór, Prince of Desmond
Published by The Black Eagle Press for The Niadh Nask

Review by The MacCarthy Mór, Prince of Desmond: This, the Count of Clandermond's latest publication, will prove to be of immense interest to members of The Niadh Nask, the dynastic Order of the Royal House of MacCarthy Mór, and indeed to general readers interested in collecting bookplates. The plates are supported by an invaluable brief and concise history of the Order, an historical examination and analysis of the more ancient bookplates illustrated, and a "Who's Who"-like catalogue providing biographical information on the individual owners and, when known, details on the artists from whom the Ex Libris were commissioned.

108 pages, illustrated card cover;
43 plates illustrating 71 black & white and 6 color plates; ISBN 0952383829
US$27 postpaid (US$32 non-US airmail)

ULSTER'S OFFICE 1552-1800
A History of the Irish Office of Arms from the Tudor Plantations to the Act of Union
by The MacCarthy Mór, Prince of Desmond
with a foreword by John P.B. Brooke-Little, Esq., CVO, MA, FSA, Clarenceux King of Arms

- The Rise of the English Heralds, Anglo-Norman and Gaelic Heraldry, & the Ireland Kings of Arms.
- The Foundation of Ulster's Office & the Development of the Duties of the Kings of Arms.
- Ulster King of Arms and the House of Lords.
- Peers & Precedence.
- The Visitations 1568-1618.
- Funeral Entries, Fees & Perquisites.
- Arms & Pedigrees.
- Ulster King of Arms & the Viceregal Court.
- Office Finances & Addresses.

• A Biographical Successional List of Ulster Kings of Arms & Athlone Pursuivants 1552-1800.
• Extensive Appendices

280+ pages, 6½" X 9½" Clothbound covers, booktext stock, Illustrated, Indexed with an extensive bibliography
US$25 postpaid (US$35 non-US Customers postpaid airmail)

GRYFONS PUBLISHERS & DISTRIBUTORS
PO Box 1899 . Little Rock . Arkansas . 72203-1899 . USA
Order online — gryfons.hypermart.net,
or fax orders to 501-834-4038